How Did They Do It?

Ashley Coates

How Did They Do It?

ISBN-13: 978-1492853138
ISBN-10: 1492853135

To Mum & Dad

.

CONTENTS

Introduction

By December 2010, Julian Dunkerton, the co-founder and CEO of Superdry, had become one of the UK's most successful retailers. Supergroup had reached a market capitalisation of £1.2 billion and the brand was rapidly expanding both in the UK and abroad, leaving many in the industry to wonder how he had got there. Meeting Julian Dunkerton at Superdry's headquarters in Cheltenham for this book it was hard to believe that he once personally travelled with his stocks of clothes from London to Hertfordshire to sell at the one shop he owned at the time. It is equally hard to imagine Rowan Williams as a young academic, scaling the perimeter fence of RAF Alconbury to protest against nuclear proliferation, or Gerard Baker, Editor of the *Wall Street Journal*, actively pursuing election as a Labour candidate for his Oxford student union.

Everyone in this book had a starting point, whether it was the origination of a business idea or a lucky break in the media or just the decision to work incredibly hard to get the top job. The contributors were deliberately picked to represent a cross section of different industries, coming from business, politics, media, sport, and the military. Collectively, they are thought to be worth over £1 billion and between them they have accumulated 4 Lordships, 4 Knighthoods, 5 CBEs, 3 OBEs and 2 MBEs. In this book they describe their careers in their own words, offering a wealth of experience, covering their motivations and personal habits, how they formulate new ideas, how they decided on the career they wanted to pursue, what regrets they have and any advice they might have for the reader. The interviews are deliberately lengthy, far longer than most newspaper or magazine interviews, providing the interviewee with an opportunity to talk about his or her life in detail as well as giving a good overall impression of the contributor. Many of the books in the business, management and leadership genres preach business lessons largely in abstract, but here the contributors take us point-by-point through the real-life scenarios they faced as they sought to establish themselves in their particular field.

Educational textbooks often have a "using this book" page after the introduction and in this instance I would urge anyone reading this not to navigate the book by picking out the most exciting sounding companies or industries but to see this as being about the individuals themselves. How a price comparison site came into being may not sound interesting at first glance but is more appealing when you know that its founder and CEO is a mother of two from Swansea who left school with just six GCSEs and is now thought to be worth roughly £95 million.

The Prince's Trust was an obvious destination for the funds raised by the book sales. The Prince's Trust was an obvious destination for the funds raised by the book sales. Since 1976, The Prince's Trust has been helping the UK's most disadvantaged young people change their lives by getting them back into education, training or employment. The Trust builds their confidence and skills so that they can identify their strengths, take responsibility for their lives, and work towards a future they can be proud of. To find out more about their vital work, please visit princes-trust.org.uk or call 0845 177 0099. I am hugely indebted to each of the contributors and their staff, all of whom donated their time free of charge.

Since I started this work in September 2012, I have often been asked if speaking to these individuals has shown up any commonalities between them. Unfortunately, the only characteristic that they all claim to have is that they are extremely hard-workers. If you wanted to read a "I can make it happen for you" kind of book you are in for a disappointment, there is not a single person here who has not fought very hard to get where they are today. Revealingly, a large number of the contributors could have retired many years ago but are working just as hard at the time of writing as they did when they first started out. Some, like Julian Fellowes, or Arlene Phillips have described themselves as workaholics. Others, such as Julian Dunkerton of Superdry and Hayley Parsons of GoCompare.com point to the desire to expand their business operations as a major source of motivation. I have deliberately intended for this book to be "open-ended", it does not claim to have all the answers, or any answers at all, but if there is one message that I hope this work has for the reader it is not to expect success to happen overnight.

Ashley Coates, London, 2013

How Did They Do It?

Alan Johnson MP

Labour Cabinet Minister 2004-2010
Member of Parliament for Hull West and Hessle 1997-

*"There is a sense that people who have come from a more privileged background have come
from a different planet and I had no real link to them at all but that would have been the
case whether I had been in politics or not, I just met more of them in politics".*

Alan Johnson held some of the most senior roles in the governments of
Tony Blair and Gordon Brown. Having been elected to Parliament in 1997, he
went on to become the Secretary of State for Work & Pensions, Trade &
Industry, Education, Health, and finally Home Secretary. Alan began his life in
absolute poverty, growing up in one of the most deprived parts of London. The
Johnson family had no central heating, no indoor toilet and his mother, Lily, was
a victim of domestic abuse. She died when Alan was just 12 years old, making
him and his sister orphans. He left school at 15 before taking up a job stacking
shelves in Tesco and becoming a postman aged 18.

His early life is a sharp contrast with the experiences of most of his
contemporaries on either side of the House of Commons. Far from being a career
politician, one of Alan's earliest pursuits was music, joining two bands, one of
which was fairly successful and played at venues around London. His dreams of a
life in music were finally ended when his guitar was stolen outside the White
Hart in Islington and he moved into a more stable career path at the Post Office.
Known for being personable and quick witted, Alan worked his way up the trade
union movement, and was elected to Parliament in 1997. In office he was in
charge of two notoriously difficult departments, the Department of Health and
the Home Office. Often inspired by the problems he had experienced in his
youth, Alan worked to reduce the overwhelming number of incapacity claimants
and improve he lives of children in care, as well as dealing with the major policy
issues of the day, such as counter-terrorism and hospital bugs.

**You started out with nothing, no contacts, no qualifications and no
particular workplace skills to mention. What personal qualities were
needed to get Alan Johnson from stacking shelves to one of the great
offices of state?**

I suppose I had an ability to write reasonably well, speak reasonably well
and argue and negotiate reasonably well. These are all attributes you needed in

the trade union movement and attributes you need in Parliament. I couldn't say it was "determination" in my case as I never set out to be a Member of Parliament from the beginning. Having said that, you do need to have a certain amount of self-confidence in order to do these things, I certainly developed that from childhood. I had help from various people, principally my English teacher, who saw something in me that others didn't seem to see so clearly.

Were there any specific experiences from your upbringing that gave you these characteristics?

I just liked reading and when you like reading you pick up a lot of the tricks of writing and how to express yourself. That love of reading was instilled in me principally by my mother, who took us down to Ladbroke Grove Library when we were just little tots. I think that has a lot to do with my success as most of what I have done I have been elected to do, rather than appointed to do.

You weren't deliberately directing yourself to be a cabinet minister from a young age but did you have a sense at all when you were growing up that you wanted to do something political?

Not political, no. I had a sense that there might be an opportunity for me to write or be a musician. I always thought that something would come up, for example, when I joined the Post Office, I started reading the Post Office staff magazine and thought "someone must write that, maybe I could transfer over to that?". So I always thought something would come up but I was pretty lethargic, I never set out to make it happen for myself. I never went and played in pubs as many musicians do off their own back to promote their work.

Could you tell me a bit more about the Area and the Inbetweens, the bands you were involved in?

The Area was just a band started by myself and two of my friends, Andrew Wiltshire and Danny Curtis. At the time Andrew and I were 16 and we thought Danny was ancient but he must have only been about 20. The three of us decided to form a band and advertised for two other band members. We had lots of gigs around London and as far out as Aylesbury College where we played to about a thousand people, that was our biggest gig. We had all our gear nicked, including my amplifier which I was paying for another two years on hire purchase. The band that then invited me to join them was much more professional, they had a manager and their own amplifiers. They were multi-racial as well which was unusual in the mid-sixties, really unusual. Once again all our gear got nicked in Islington, including my fabulous guitar so I just could not go on. By that time I was about to get married and thought I would get a steady occupation so I joined the Post Office.

You have talked about your book being a biography of your parents, Steve and Lily and your sister, Linda. The book has been widely noted for not having an overtly political message. What message would you like people to take away from it?

I just wanted to tell a story about these two incredible women, my mother and my sister, but when a parent dies very young, you don't know them very well, so the act of recreating and in a sense being their biographer, was the real challenge for me. I wanted to make it interesting and record that postwar life in Britain in the 50s which is often thought of as a prosperous time. I was in one of the poorest areas because North Kensington, right back to the 18th century was a very poor area. So it was about telling the story of the location, the Notting Hill riots, the murder of Kelso Cochrane and then the experience of being in a school on King's Road during the 1960s. If I wanted the reader to be left with any message it was that this is a well written book and that they understand the lives of people like Lily.

Did you ever feel like you were sorting out a particular issue during your ministerial career directly due to the experiences you had in your youth?

A few, yes, at Work and Pensions we were dealing with millions of people that had been consigned to a life on benefits in order to bring the unemployment statistics down. The numbers on incapacity benefit had gone up from around 700,000 in 1979 to 2.6 million in 1997. Everyone knew why that was, it was because after they left the shipyards or steel works as they shut down, they were ushered onto incapacity benefit. It wasn't a lot of money but it was higher than Jobseeker's Allowance and you didn't have to keep trying to get work. So in areas like Strathclyde, which was a particular hotspot, people were pushed to the margin of their own lives. When we started saying to people that we would change the law so that people could go back to work without having to go to the back of the queue, people were beating down the door to have the opportunity.

Another was education and looked after children [children in public care] who had a terrible time and who I could quite easily have turned out to be. Half a per cent of the child population are looked after children, but they go on to make up 20 per cent of the prison population. They were being put into care too easily, they were being moved around too much and pushed out too young.

Those were the areas where I could relate what was going on to my own experiences.

Some politicians seem to get affected by the "hubris of power" after a few years in office. Margaret Thatcher is perhaps a good example of this. Did you find that you needed to ground yourself as the years went by?

I didn't have that chip in my mental make-up! No, I didn't have to ground myself, the people around me would do that anyway. You have special advisors as a cabinet minister and they are generally people you know and they wouldn't let me get above my station. There are many MPs, on the Conservative side as well, who find the way that some of our colleagues treat people who they consider to be menial, or people who are not very important to their progression, really appalling. I've heard stories of very senior politicians going on television and being very keen to chat to the presenters but their rudeness to the make-up team and the staff is extraordinary. You either have that in you or you don't.

Most of the characters in the House of Commons do have an innate and very robust self-confidence that has been nurtured through experiences that you wouldn't have had.

You get these sorts of characters that you are talking about but you wouldn't be surrounded by them. They were there and they and to be dealt with. I wish I had gone to university, I think university gives you a certain confidence, it certainly gives you a network and what used to be called a "trained mind". I was Higher Education Minister for a time and it was never a case of saying to people "I got where I am without university", I was always arguing with young people that they could go to university and that they should aspire to go to university. There is a sense that people who have come from a more privileged background have come from a different planet and I had no real link to them at all but that would have been the case whether I had been in politics or not, I just met more of them in politics.

John Prescott gets quite hung up on the idea that there is a huge gulf between him and people that came from different economic backgrounds.

Yes, why was John so prickly about all that? I think it was because he got a really bad press. It's a chicken or the egg question. He used to get people like Nicholas Soames, who whenever he saw him would say, "gin and tonic please, waiter". I never had that, there were a few people who would use the fact that I was a postman as a reason why I shouldn't be in the job. I would get the odd letter saying "that is what would happen when you put a postman in a cabinet position". But in my experience that was a minority. John suffered more of that, perhaps because of the age he came through Parliament and because he was Deputy Prime Minister.

At the beginning of his autobiography, John Major wrote about how he had mentally prepared himself for no longer being Prime Minister way before he left office. He realised he would need to adapt to a time without the buzz of government, constant news interest, chauffeurs and the like. How did you prepare yourself for leaving office?

John could see the writing on the wall a long time before the '97 election. We should have seen the writing on the wall and certainly the odds were that we were going to be out of office but in the end it was a hung parliament. I thought we might continue in government and when it turned out to be a hung parliament I thought we may go into government with the Lib Dems. So it was very sudden, though probably less sudden for a Home Secretary because you keep protection for a while. You keep the car and all that whereas most ministers are shown the door and that's it. You even ring your old private office two hours after you had lost government and whereas they would have said "Hello, Alan Johnson's office", they say "this is Theresa May's place". I was a bit at sea for a while and I hated shadowing the position. We had all agreed to shadow ourselves so one moment I was Home Secretary the next I was Shadow Home Secretary.

It must have been immensely dislocating.

It was awful and I hadn't prepared myself for that. John Major didn't have to in a way because he knew he was out as you don't go anywhere after you have been Prime Minister. It's Tony Blair's famous phrase, "when you are in opposition you wake up every morning and think about what you are going to say whereas in government you wake up and think about what you are going to do".

What advice would you give to some who is interested in a career in politics and government?

Get some experience of the world under your belt and don't try to do it too young, I think there is a push back against that now. Consider being a councillor or doing something voluntarily for your community while you are getting on with your career. Do something that means you are dealing with people and representing people. You can have an inverted snobbery about these things, William Pitt the Younger was 24 when he became Prime Minister, but that's when people dropped down dead when they were 34. It is very hard for people to think that someone so young can be in Parliament making decisions about people's lives when they haven't got much experience of life. Charles Kennedy came in very young and he would admit that he couldn't contribute as much as an older person could.

Alastair Fothergill

Natural History film-maker
Producer, *BBC Planet Earth, The Blue Planet*,
Executive Producer, *Frozen Planet*.

*"You could get a shot like having an elephant in the desert and you would pull back and
pull back and pull back and you would just see this animal, this enormous animal, the
world's largest vegetarian, in a world without a single blade of grass".*

The producer behind some of the most visually impressive and
commercially successful natural history films ever made produced his first natural
history film, *On the Okavango*, while he was still a student at university. The film
looked at the experiences of Alastair and his fellow students in an area around the
Okavango Delta in Botswana and although it "wasn't a terribly good film", it gave
Alastair the idea to pursue natural history filmmaking as a career. He made a
number of short films of his own before he joined the BBC's world-renowned
Natural History Unit as a researcher in 1983 working on *The Really Wild Show*. He
then went on to work on the major Attenborough series *Wildlife on One* and *The
Trials of Life* then produced *Life in the Freezer*. Alastair accepted the role of Head
of the Natural History Unit while he was still in his thirties and though he initially
found it difficult to not be directly involved in programme-making, the
opportunity to oversee the output of such a successful arm of BBC factual
production proved immensely rewarding.

Anyone that has ever wondered how the images from these series were
captured will find that it is just as difficult as it looks. Each of Alastair's three
major series took several years to produce and some of the more challenging
sequences, such as filming snow leopards, took up many months of man hours
before any usable footage was actually recorded. In total, *Planet Earth's* 71 camera
operators spent roughly 2000 days in the field, covering 204 locations in 62
countries. It was the most expensive documentary the BBC had commissioned to
date but paid back its budget through DVD and foreign rights sales, becoming the
highest selling factual DVD ever made. Alastair left the Natural History Unit in
2012 to pursue his own projects. *Chimpanzee*, a feature-length documentary
directed by Alastair and produced by Disney Nature was released in cinemas in
April 2013.

**Your first film, *On the Okavango*, was produced while your were
studying at Durham, what was this film about and how useful was it**

18

to you in getting to the next stage in your career?

At the time the BBC was running a competition that was named after a cameraman called Mick Birk who had died on the south face of Everest. It was a bi-annual competition where the BBC would choose six expeditions, often university students but not always, and we went off with cameras and sound equipment and then judges came in and chose the winner. The Okavango is a place in Botswana, it's a beautiful area about the size of Wales, and we didn't see another white person for the whole period. We made a film about our adventure and to be honest it wasn't a terribly good film, but it was very good for me. I knew from a very small age that I wanted to work with animals, I chose to study Zoology, and I thought I might have been a research biologist but it was while making this film that I realised it was a wonderful way to get to work with animals. I went on to make a couple of films and when I came to apply for a job at the Natural History Unit in Bristol, the fact that I had that experience on my CV was great as there weren't many graduates in those days that had that sort of experience.

You made quite a few films while you were still a student.

Yes I then did some work for BBC Look North, I had a camera I borrowed off a friend and I made a film about wild goats in the Lake District. I also made a film about the university, a newsreel film which was shown in the Students' Union. In those days before DVDs the Students' Union would show a film every Saturday night and we decided we would do a newsreel, just like they did during the war, which would be shown alongside the feature film they were showing. We shot that locally and we paid for that with advertising from local shops that we shot. It all inspired me to do more work in film.

Having joined the Natural History Unit in 1992 you then worked your way up the production hierarchy

My very first job was actually on the BBC Wildlife magazine as a researcher, that brought me to Bristol and then I moved into the *Really Wild Show*. I did children's programmes for five years before working on *Wildlife on One* and then I joined David Attenborough as a producer on *The Trials of Life* which was his third big series. I then managed to persuade them to let me do the first series of my own which was *Life in the Freezer* and literally half way through that job I was offered the role of Head of the Natural History Unit. To be honest at the time, aged 32, I wanted to be out in the field but a lot of my colleagues encouraged me to do it so I did it. So I took it and that afternoon I flew into the Falklands and sailed to South Georgia and I remember sailing on yacht around the

Falklands and thinking, "what on Earth am I doing, why have I given up all this?" but actually it was really challenging to be head of the department at that age. The Natural History Unit is a really special place. Almost all the people who work there have a real passion for their work and it was a real privilege to manage these very passionate people.

Something that made *Planet Earth* and *Frozen Planet* really special was the utilisation of new technologies and techniques that helped tell the stories in a refreshingly cinematic style, could you outline some of the technologies you employed to give *Planet Earth* that really cinematic feel?

People often talk about technology and I can understand why because they are crucial and natural history is about revelation, it's about showing things that people haven't seen before. To a certain extent technology is very important, for example in *The Private Life of Plants* it was very essential that new technology such as the time-lapse was there because plants do a lot but they do it very slowly. So technology makes plants come alive and reveals that behaviour through time-lapse. The other major technology we employed was something called Cine-Flex which was a camera on a gyroscope on a helicopter. We could stabilise a very powerful camera in an airborne position and that meant we could get animals in good quality on the ground from a height. We could shoot the whole sequence from the air and get all the action and not disturb the animals. But actually the reason why all that worked well for *Planet Earth* is that it worked editorially very well for *Planet Earth*. You could get a shot like having an elephant in the desert and you would pull back and pull back and pull back and you would just see this animal, this enormous animal, the world's largest vegetarian, in a world without a single blade of grass.

I think the success of *The Blue Planet* and *Planet Earth* is, yes to a certain extent, it is cinematic and certainly the vision was to do that but that isn't just technology. What makes it cinematic is the whole style, the editing, the pace of the programme, the whole approach. One of the things about *Planet Earth* is it had half the number of cuts of the average 50-minute film at that time. It had around 250 cuts in a 50-minute show. Many shows have 700 plus and I remember people saying, "do you think it's going to be too slow for BBC1?" and I thought if every shot is a Rembrandt and you have real, real confidence in your images then it will work and that is why it felt epic but it's not just the technology. The technology tail should not wag the dog.

It's the narrative that's driving it.

It's the editorial and the narrative and it's the emotions you want to engender in the audience that are important. If you can achieve that by various techniques and technologies then fine, I actually think in certain areas of natural history, the technology often gets between you and the viewer.

Continuing with the way the story unfolds, the three projects that you are best known for, *Planet Earth*, *The Blue Planet* and *Frozen Planet* each took several years to complete and required multiple camera teams in locations all over the globe, how do you maintain a consistent narrative, or sense of story, when you are working over such huge timescales and with such disparate teams?

We work very hard on that. In the first year we usually don't do very much filming, we do a lot of research and a lot of discussion of the scripts. The series I made were designed for BBC1 and I always say to my teams that if you can't tell why the series is special in one line then it's not going to work, it's "*Planet Earth*: as you have never seen it before", that was the strap-line, "*The Blue Planet*: so far we have only scratched the surface", "*Frozen Planet*: a world behind imagination". Then you make sure that there is a logic to the order of the programme, *Frozen Planet* had a seasonal story line because that is the big story in the polar part of the world and then in terms of ordering, I consider whether, if there is no narration, would the images themselves tell a story?

You need a very simple storyline that builds through the programme and finally we talk about what we call the jigsaw story line, and that is, when all the bits of the jigsaw come together, do you see the whole picture? I think if you make these series of really broad appeal they have to have entry points for different types of people, there are some people who just look at the pictures and go, "wow". There are others who want more, they want to learn something, they want to get more out of the programme and that is what we mean by the jigsaw storyline. We just review it the whole time, we write the programme at the beginning and every month I would sit down with the producers and review how they are doing, how they are spending their money, constantly questioning the sequences we are doing and whether an episode is going to run long enough.

How controlled can you make it? A lot of the footage can't be anticipated such as that moment in *The Blue Planet* where you were filming the bait ball and suddenly a Sei Whale comes out of nowhere and appears to swallow the whole thing. That sort of event seems to happen a lot.

I would say it's about risk management, you know you have a certain amount of money, you know you have 50 minutes of air time. As *The Blue Planet* and *Planet Earth* have sold very well internationally, I have been able to turn around to BBC Worldwide, who provide almost a third of the budget, and say, "I need a very big budget" and they always say "why do you need so much money?" and I say "well you need the money to fail". A perfect example would be the snow leopard we filmed in Planet Earth, it had never been filmed before and we had two eight-week shoots where we didn't film a single frame. For the average *Natural World* shoot, if they did an eight-week shoot and shot nothing, the budget would have been blown. So the way I analysed it with the producers is you should make sure for any one show you have got at least half of the sequences which are pretty predictable. Then at the same time people want to see new things, so there are a number of sequences which are Holy Grail type sequences and are very risky.

Staying on the funding structure, the three major Planet series were each co-funded by the BBC and Discovery Channel, could you explain how the funding and distribution rights worked for these programmes?

This is approximate but about a third of the budget comes from the BBC and about a third of the funding comes from co-production in the US. Up until now that has always been Discovery because the BBC has an output deal with Discovery. Another third comes from BBC Worldwide, the commercial arm of the BBC, they basically sell the rights to the rest of the world. *Planet Earth* made a lot of money for the BBC because their contribution was easily paid for by the television sales and it sold five million DVDs in America. It is the highest-selling factual DVD in history. What's great is that is all reinvested, it doesn't go to shareholders as it would were it a private company, it gets reinvested into other programmes that might not be so commercial.

You joined the Natural History Unit in 1983 and you have been able to see many different parts of the world change since, to what extent have you got a sense of the natural world being in decline?

I have rarely been back to the same place. The only place I have been back to a number of times are the polar regions and those are very interesting areas because they are wildernesses, particularly in the Antarctic, man's direct influence has been very small. There is no rainforest to cut down, there is no pollution, there are no overpopulation issues but there is absolutely no doubt that you can see global warming. Global warming is something that is very difficult to see usually but you can definitely see it in the Antarctic. In South Georgia there was an explorer who worked with Shackleton called Hurley who took some beautiful black-and-white photographs at the beginning of the last century of the glacier in South Georgia. In the early nineties when I went back with David Attenborough we got David to walk in front of exactly the same glacier. For *Frozen Planet* again we lined up the cameras exactly how the original photographs were framed and when you mix those images together you can see the glaciers retreating up the mountain. The other thing that is interesting are different types of penguin are adapted to different amounts of cold. The deep south penguin, that's the penguin that likes the pack ice and does well in the cold, it's called the Adele penguin, it's colonies along the Antarctic peninsula have decreased and they have been replaced increasingly with penguins from further north. That is clear evidence of change.

I think the other location where there is clear evidence of change is in the rainforest. I haven't been back to Borneo since the nineties but David has and you can really see how the rainforest has been cut down to provide palm oil. Another place you can really see huge change is underwater. Many of the sequences we filmed for *Blue Planet* would be very difficult to do today just because there aren't as many of these habitats anymore. So I am in absolutely no doubt that these changes are happening.

Allan Niblo

Film producer, co-founder Vertigo Films

"When I started in the business there were only ten real film schools in the country, now there are thousands of students graduating every year. It's a dream job, it is a job that many people desire but it's a Herculian effort to get seen by a wide audience".

Today the company that Allan Niblo co-founded in 2002 is one of the most successful independent production companies in Europe, releasing *The Football Factory*, *The Sweeney*, *Streetdance* and *Horrid Henry* to commercial and critical acclaim. Its productions reflect an interest in developing homegrown talent and Vertigo has backed a number of emerging actors and directors who were just starting to make the move into cinema. The impression many people have of the film industry is one of red carpet award ceremonies, glamorous actors and the romance of putting together a great film, but the realities of getting a film financed, shot and distributed are very far from romantic. The margins for British independent film in particular are very tight, few producers make much money from the industry, and just getting distributed is, in Allan's words "a Herculian effort".

Allan's beginnings in the industry are unusual. He completed a competitive training program for a major bank, RBS, but after four years in finance, Allan turned it all in to become, a "skate bum". If anything you might have expected Allan to move into the business side of film, working in international sales or finance, but the day he passed his final banking exams he flew to California to get a taste for the way things are done there before returning to the UK to make promotional videos for local musicians. Back in the UK he performed a number of roles- film student, cameraman, director of photography, film lecturer - before getting what you might call his "big break", producing *Human Traffic*. Starring Danny Dyer and John Simm, and eventually bought by Miramax, the film put Allan "on the map".

Today Allan oversees Vertigo's vertically-integrated operations at its office in North London and produces several feature-length films every year. The company covers production, post-production (including 3D films), as well as distribution. His advice to anyone interested in joining him in the film business is to make sure you really want to do it, having a love of the moving image is key, but also to be prepared to work extremely hard as nothing will be handed to you on a plate.

There can't be many people in British independent film who trained as bankers, how did you end up in a bank and why did you leave?

My best subjects at school were Maths and Physics so I got As in all that and went straight from that thinking the best route to take was to go to the Royal Bank of Scotland. I got on an accelerated training program they put me on to do the industry's banking exams so I passed all of them in four years and literally the day after I passed them I moved to California. I was skating a lot and playing in punk bands and it was the exact opposite of banking so the day I passed I realised that it was not for me so I did the polar-opposite and became a skate bum.

Was it not quite difficult taking yourself out of that solid career path and doing something completely different?

It was a massive thing because my dad was really disappointed and the bank never forgave me because they spent a lot of money putting me through that training program and there were a thousand applicants for it and only two places. At the time, back when I was younger, especially where I came from, if you got an apprenticeship or a traineeship, you stayed with that company for life, it wasn't like the transience that's around these days. So it was a big jump.

So how did your parents react?

They weren't happy, to be honest with you, but I knew I didn't want to work in a bank for the rest of my life.

Was that where the direct connection to what you are doing now started? Being in California and thinking: "I should be doing this"?

Yes, exactly, it was a real light bulb moment, it was where I really felt: "the moving image, what a wonderful thing". It was literally - "I'm coming from a small town in Scotland", I wanted to experience California and the opposite side of the world and live the dream life and see what I could discover out there. I had been into movies, since Channel 4 started in the 80s, I was always into Turkish and Iranian cinema and Russian cinema but I never thought I could have a career in movies in any shape or form. The school's careers teachers back in Scotland just laughed at you back then.

What was the next step?

I bought a video camera and started making pop promos for local bands. It started to look good after a while and I applied to undergraduate film school and I got into Newport Film School. I spent two years training there, put a good show reel together, applied to the National Film School and got in as a cameraman there.

Is film school a route you would recommend to someone today?

I had a great time at the NFTS, it's one of the elite film schools of the world, it is an amazing place to meet people and be inspired by people and to learn. But it's not the only route, plenty of people can take other routes. Loving movies is the most important thing.

What was the route to founding your own production company?

So, I went from the National Film School where I was a Director of Photography, to making commercials in television for about two or three years doing that making quite good money. Then I decided I didn't want to be a DoP anymore so I went back to education as a film lecturer at university, the University of Wales, spent four years there and just as those four years were coming to an end and I was looking for something to do, I met a student and I said "let's make a film". He was only 24 at the time and couldn't believe I wanted to make a film with him and that became *Human Traffic*. I managed to raise the money for that as a producer and it was a big hit. We sold it to Miramax at the time and it put me on the map.

Was that the moment you realised you were actually now in the industry on a serious level?

Yes, that was my real entry point to the film industry. I had worked in commercials and television for a bit but that was the entry into the movie business. The film went to all these film festivals all over the world and I got to meet a whole range of people.

It's interesting you talk about meeting people because the industry does have a bit of a reputation for the whole "it's not what you know, it's who you know" sort of thing, have you encountered much in the way of nepotism in your career?

Nepotism does exist but nepotism exists in all walks of life I don't think it's peculiar to the film business, one thing's for sure is if you have got talent it will show through. You can be given the opportunity but you've still got to prove yourself by doing it.

The cream will rise to the top.

Exactly whether you are a good director or a good cameraman, your talent will shine through. Someone can open the door for you but you have to perform.

How did *The Football Factory* come to be produced?

After *Human Traffic* I bought the rights to *Football Factory* and then we asked Nick Love to get involved because I had seen his first film, which I loved, *Goodbye Charlie Brown*. Nick at the time had been in development and he hadn't yet come across his next film after *Goodbye Charlie Brown* so when we approached him he loved the subject matter and a few months later wrote a screenplay and that was it.

In terms of selecting the projects you want to pursue, what do you look for as a producer?

Vertigo is about two things, it's about establishing a really great business, so making a mark in the landscape in film and being a sustainable company that's taking risks and being adventurous. In that respect we are a film company and a distribution company, we jointly own a sales company with Channel 4 and Ingenious called Protagonist. We've also got a post-production facility that does state-of-the-art post-production in Berlin and we've got a 3D company. So we are being quite adventurous in terms of how we set the business up and that's very exciting.

Separate to that, in terms of the actual movies that we decide to produce, it's about a range of product. I'd say we are known for a commercial eye, which is quite a rare thing in British film actually. It's only more recently that material is becoming more commercial in this country, for a long time it was deemed a dirty word. We are doing a range of films for family entertainment, like *Horrid Henry*, *Streetdance* and *The Wombles*, all the way to bold experimental work like *Monsters*, where there's no script, there's one guy who has to do all this CGI and yet is able to make a film that has an impact on the world stage. Or *Bronson*, a prison drama, an elevated-genre movie, is how I would describe it, all the way through to big commercial films like *The Sweeney* and bigger projects that we are setting up at the moment.

How do you divide up your time within the business with such a lot going on? How do you know what to prioritise?

There's quite a lot of housekeeping to be done running your own company. We now have about 55 members of staff across three companies and for each company whether it's Protagonist or Post Republic or Vertigo, it takes time. We each have different methods of working within the company. Nick is obviously a writer-director, concentrating on his own projects, and writes and directs projects for other people potentially as well, whereas James and I are very much producers, we each have projects that we work on individually but we always collaborate. Rupert runs the distribution but also produces as well. Him and I have a close working relationship over the product, from distribution to production.

Do you feel that the emergence of the internet is creating opportunities for filmmakers or actually eating into your end of the business, the extra low-budget YouTube films and the like?

Nothing can eat into the business because of the dominance of Hollywood in the cinemas, and in television and DVD as well. There is only a small piece of the pie left for everyone else and it is up to us to make that pie bigger. If you're a filmmaker now you've never had a better opportunity because not only can you pick up a video camera, which is accessible to everybody, you can edit it on your laptop and you can find your music online. You can do the distribution yourself and you can get yourself noticed via a website so the entire process is at your fingertips and it's the first time making movies has been like that. It's been democratised in a really clever way I think. I have yet to see many people take advantage of that in this country, they are still looking for big budgets to enable them to make their movies but some of the movies that have inspired us didn't have that. For example, we made *In Search of a Midnight Kiss*, which was made for $15,000. There was a director who was frustrated in the studio system and a bunch of actor friends who said, "to hell with it, let's make a movie now" and picked up a camera, started working on it and a few months later, a film popped out that got exceptional reviews.

So if you were starting now, how would you go about establishing yourself in the film industry?

If I was starting now I would be really interested in alternative business models. When Vertigo first started up we got a lot of attention by being the first company to shoot digitally, the first company to micro-finance films, the first company to set up a wholly integrated post-production facility. We were the first company to work with MySpace on a movie, we were seen as pioneers, trying things out. Not all of it worked but at least we were seen as new and fresh and cutting-edge, that goes a long way in the business if you've got a perception of freshness. So if you're saying, "how would you start now?" I'd say, look at a fresh angle that will get you noticed and they're out there, modes of distribution, massive companies whose advertising is restricted that might want to make movies to promote their products, online distribution and new modes of making movies with things like go-pro cameras. Never before has there been a better chance to make films that are low budget and appeal to the masses.

You would do this right now, starting from scratch, say as a student coming out of university?

Yes, absolutely. I'd be talking to businesses like Red Bull and Relentless Energy drinks. I'd be looking at ways you can connect businesses with an audience the way that viral videos can. How do I own all the rights and keep it all for myself? How do I break the traditional models that exist out there? If I were starting out again, I would be looking at all of that.

Most young people who are interested in TV and film are recommended to take the runner route, starting at the bottom making tea, is a strategy you would support? I guess it depends on the area you are interested in.

So if someone wanted career advice coming out of school? It's a difficult question to answer that. When I started in the business there were only ten real film schools in the country, now there are thousands of students graduating every year. It's a dream job, it is a job that many people desire but it's a Herculian effort to get seen by a wide audience. You've got to have absolute determination to find out what your goal is and how you achieve your goal. If you are a director the best thing to do is make an amazing short film that wins loads of awards and blows people away at festivals, you need one or two of them. If you are exceptional in that area and rise above the pack, you'll get noticed by the FilmFours, the BFIs, the Vertigos, we'll pick that up. We're looking for the hottest talent.

Amanda Berry OBE

Chief Executive, BAFTA

"I'd produced BAFTA's awards ceremonies for Scottish Television and was passionate about what they were trying to achieve. I just thought, "I have to go for that job" and for the second time in my life I was prepared to take a substantial pay cut to do a job that I really believed in".

When Amanda took up the Chief Executive role at BAFTA in 2000, the Academy was suffering from lack of interest and lack of funds. Although it was still hosting the annual awards ceremonies that it is best known for, the organisation had gradually lost touch with both the public and much of its own membership. Amanda is widely recognised as having turned BAFTA around. Since the start of her tenure, the prospects for the Academy have increased dramatically. Moving the Film Awards ceremony from March to before the Oscars required a huge amount of work but it now means that the awards are seen as part of the New Year awards season. The charitable functions of the organisation have also increased, going from around four events a month excluding the awards ceremonies to around 250 events a year, most of which are accessible to the public.

It's an impressive track record for Amanda, who describes herself as a "dry cleaner's daughter from North Yorkshire". She has gone from interning at a Newcastle newspaper to running one of the most prestigious organisations in film in what has been a winding route through PR, television and talent agencies. Success in the media is typically characterised as being a case of "it's not what you know, it's who you know", but when Amanda was looking for her first job, she knew no-one. Nor did she really know exactly what she wanted to do. But Amanda did know that she wanted to be somewhere in the creative industries and set about finding an opening, writing letters and making applications. Amanda's guiding light has always been finding jobs that she enjoys, moving on from most of her posts once she has felt she has made a worthwhile contribution.

Amanda joined BAFTA as Head of Development and Events in 1998 and became Chief Executive in 2000. She was awarded an OBE for services to the film and television industries in 2009 and entered the Telegraph's 100 Most Powerful Women in Britain list in 2010. In 2012, she made the Times' British Film Power 100 and the Evening Standard's 1000 Most Influential People in London lists.

Could you outline how you came to be involved in media organisations, starting from university?

I was at Newcastle Polytechnic, studying Business Studies and Graphic Design and each year you had to go out on a placement. In the first year, I worked on a local newspaper, the Evening Chronicle. I think they thought I was a little bit different because I had bright blue hair and I was a bit of a punk. They were just fabulous with me – so supportive and encouraging. While I was at the Poly, I was a member of the Entertainments Committee and Editor of the student newspaper, but I didn't ever really know what I wanted to do. I don't know where it came from, but for my second-year placement I decided I wasn't going to go to one that the polytechnic had organised locally; I wanted to work in a PR department in a television company.

Following your instincts I suppose?

I don't know. I wrote to 15 television companies and I was very lucky that one of them said yes. I worked across the PR Department and the Publicity Department at Thames Television and couldn't have been better supported, and I ended up staying for six months. I loved being in London and I thought if I moved back to Newcastle to complete my course, I would struggle to make the move again to London. I didn't have many qualifications, but I had shorthand and typing, so I applied for secretarial roles and, again, I was very lucky. It was a time when pretty much every role I applied for, I was offered. The job I eventually went for was what I have always referred to as "second junior assistant from the left" at a theatrical agency. I was the 53rd person who was interviewed for the job and I got it. The only reason I knew anything about theatrical agents was because my job in the press office at Thames involved forwarding fan mail to people's agents, so I had a bit of a clue as to what they did. Within a year of being there, I became an assistant to the owner. Duncan Heath Associates was quite small when I joined, but we were taken over by a large American company and started to grow. I became a company director and started spent a lot of time in LA and New York, as well as London. I did that for six years before wanting to do something else. I have to be absolutely in love with what I do and when that starts to wane, it is time for me to do something else.

I took three months out to decide what to do next. I then worked at LWT for a couple of years, doing everything from Telethon to the Royal Variety Performance. In 1990, my husband's job took him to Glasgow and I started working for Scottish Television. It was a bit of a culture shock to be really honest; I went from being at LWT - where you didn't work across different departments - to a much smaller television company, where as a producer you worked across numerous genres from features to documentary to entertainment, and this included BAFTA's awards ceremonies.

In 1998, I saw an advert for Head of Development and Events at BAFTA. I'd produced BAFTA's awards ceremonies for Scottish Television and was passionate about what they were trying to achieve. I just thought, "I have to go for that job" and for the second time in my life I was prepared to take a substantial pay cut to do a job that I really believed in. After three interviews I got the job and started in October '98. I was very lucky that I was starting at the right time; there was a will to grow and develop the organisation, following a period of challenging financial times. I became Chief Executive in December 2000, after at first turning the job down. I ran all the awards ceremonies and I thought it was the best job at BAFTA and I didn't want to leave that behind. The Chairman at the time said to me, "If you can stop talking for long enough, Amanda, and listen, I'll explain how you can still do your old job and hire someone to manage other parts of the business." So I hired a Chief Operating Officer and together we started to make the changes that you see in the organisation today. Did I tell you I talk a lot?

What sort of changes were you looking to achieve when you got into the organisation?

The organisation had struggled financially, so it was all about survival - delivering what it had to deliver but doing it at absolute minimum cost: with a very small staff and a very small budget. I believed that by introducing the right commercial partners into the Academy they could help us develop and grow. Now we work with 70-plus commercial partners, everyone from EE, the title sponsor for the Film Awards and our partner for 16 years, to Audi, who are the official car for the Academy - brands that share our values and understand what BAFTA stands for. It was also about looking at our priorities for the organisation. We are an educational charity, but at the turn of the millennium our events were primarily membership focused. Over the last year we produced close to 250 events that were accessible to the members and public facing. Our events range from how to make a short film and how to market it, to lectures and masterclasses covering film, television and video games, as well as mentoring schemes.

The time was also right to evaluate the awards ceremonies. The year I arrived, the Film and Television Awards became separate ceremonies and yet the Film Awards were still in April. Looking at the global Film Awards calendar, that made no sense whatsoever because our Awards came a number of weeks after the Oscars and we weren't in that window when the world was looking at film. We spent a lot of time talking to the film industry about moving the Film Awards, asking where the issues were and how the industry could support us. In 2001 we moved the Film Awards to February and since then they have grown dramatically, from an event that was broadcast just in the UK to an event that is shown in every major territory in the world. It all comes down to belief - believing in our heritage, and our brand and growing and developing it to make sure we were properly representing film, television and video games and that our membership reflected those industries. We had a very loyal membership but people new to the industry weren't necessarily thinking about joining BAFTA.

I wanted to develop the BAFTA brand - an amazing brand - one that was already recognised widely, and take it to where it is today. But I honestly didn't think when I started that I would be here 15 years later. I thought maybe after three or four years I would have done all I wanted to do and it would be time to do something else, but my ambitions for the organisation possess no limits and I am just as passionate about BAFTA today as I was when I first started.

You are often singled out as a "woman of achievement" and you have acquired a number of awards, such as Woman of the Year and getting onto the Woman of Inspiration and Enterprise list. How much do you see yourself as being ostensibly a "woman of business"? These sorts of awards almost take the angle that the careers of the people they recognise have been defined by the post-holders being women. How much do you feel that has influenced you?

I think being a woman has benefited me hugely. As a woman you can say "I've got a gut feeling about this" or "my instinct is" and nobody looks at you oddly, but these aren't things you would necessarily hear a man say very often. I have been very lucky. I have been given a free rein to take risks and take chances. Circumstances and colleagues have allowed me to be me. I have never felt that I needed to play at politics or present myself in a certain way. I used to think, "I haven't achieved what I have achieved because I am a woman; I have achieved it because of who I am". Then it struck me how fortunate I have been and how I have been supported by a lot of people, so I now feel it is my duty to support other women and I am very happy to do so.

I have a confident exterior, but I am not necessarily as confident as I look. Men seem innately to have more confidence. I always say to people that everything is possible and I really believe that. I am a real workaholic and I am really lucky that I have got jobs that make the most of my skills. I have also recognised when a job has come to the end of its natural term and I have been able to find the next job that has challenged and excited me. The awards I've gained are not just for me but for my team, and so when I got my OBE for services to the film and television industries, the first thing I did was throw a party at BAFTA, to thank everyone who had been on that 'journey' with me.

Thinking about support again, film and TV are two horrifically difficult industries to get into and seem to be increasingly so. What would you say to someone who is interested in a career in either of those industries?

They are incredibly broad sectors. Try and identify the area within the industry you are interested in. You could be great at maths and become a film production accountant, be creative and be better suited to the crafts. You won't always know immediately, so if you are not sure where you want to be, but you know that the creative industries are something you want to be in, then try to find a job as a runner, or an internship. There is an internship programme here at BAFTA which I am very supportive of because starting out I got my foot in the door through a work placement. Most people are genuinely supportive of the next generation of talent and if you write to them and say, "I need your guidance", I hope people would help. So use every contact you've got, read and research as much as you can. If you are going into an interview, expect that they are going to ask you, "What's your favourite TV show?", "What's your favourite film, and why?" Show them you have a passion for the industry. Use every possible way in you can find, and that can be as simple as writing loads of letters to people and hoping they reply!

Arlene Phillips CBE

Dancer, choreographer, TV personality

*"I put my success down to passion, determination,
drive and the amazing support of my family".*

The choreographer behind some of the best known musicals on the West End began her career in a more humble setting, practicing dance moves on the floor of her parent's house in Manchester. Arlene's conviction that dance was her calling came at a young age and she was fortunate in having parents that were keen to grow her talent. Despite her family's financial hardship, they were keen to see Arlene succeed and they began to send her to ballet classes at her local dance school. A remarkable break came when Arlene found herself babysitting for the renowned film director, Ridley Scott, who gave her the job of choreographing a commercial he was directing.

Arlene caused a stir in the 1970s when she began producing Hot Gossip, an innovative dance group that courted plaudits and controversy in equal measure with its risqué dance moves. She had seen a need for the kind of dancing that was going on in night clubs to be represented on the stage and Hot Gossip gave her the worldwide recognition needed to take her career to the next level. Throughout the 80s, Arlene choreographed music videos for Aretha Franklin, Elton John, the Bee Gees and Queen amongst others. Less well-known is her work as the choreographer behind *Monty Python's The Meaning of Life* and episodes within the *Benny Hill* and *Kenny Everett Shows*. She also went on to choreograph major West End productions.

Outside of choreography, Arlene is best known as having been a judge on both *Strictly Come Dancing?* and *So You Think You Can Dance?* Her professional, firm-but-fair, approach was widely commended. Arlene received an OBE in 2004 and a CBE in 2012. She has won an Emmy and a BAFTA and has received several nominations for Tony Awards, Olivier Awards and National Broadway Awards.

You grew up in Manchester and wanted to be a dancer from a young age. How would you characterise your upbringing and were you encouraged to follow your interests?

I always knew I wanted to dance. My parents were passionate about dance, especially ballet, and although there was little money, they did everything they could to send me to dance classes and make my dreams come true.

One of your early "breaks" came after you babysat for Ridley Scott's children. How did you end up babysitting for Ridley Scott and what did this lead to?

I arrived in London with nothing and nowhere to stay, and by chance a wonderful jazz teacher I was studying with was a friend of Ridley Scott's and knew he had a place I could live in return for babysitting for him. After a couple of months, he asked me to choreograph a Lyons Maid ice cream commercial he was directing, as he knew I was a dancer and I guess he thought all dancers could choreograph! The rest, as they say, is history.

Your reputation really took off with Hot Gossip in the late 1970s. Could you describe what the dance scene was like at the time and how Hot Gossip managed to gain the appeal it had?

Hot Gossip, the dance group I created, changed dance on TV forever because they were the first dance group who were racially mixed, didn't smile and were very, very sexy. Before that, all television dancers had a smile on their face or were miming to the songs. I loved the london scene of nightclubs and anarchy at the time and wanted to put this into dance. This was also reflected in the costumes they wore, as one of the dancers worked in a a sex shop part time, and as the group was so poor anything free was all we could afford!

How much room for maneuver do you get when you are choreographing a major West End production? Do you feel constrained at all by what audience expectations and the producers want to see or are you able to do some really different performances?

When I choreograph a musical I try not to think about audience expectations as I always have my own vision of what I want the choreography to be, and how it can work with the story. I also work very closely alongside the director and his overall vision of the piece to can link everything together. There are however often some very demanding producers, and of course what they see for the production might not always be what you originally envisaged so there might sometimes be a lot of last minute changes.

Musical theatre is a notoriously tough business, with tight deadlines, huge budgets and considerable physical demands on actors and choreographers. What would you say has been your biggest theatrical choreographing challenge?

The biggest challenge I have faced in musical theatre, and continue to face is finding performers for *Starlight Express*. The show is performed entirely on roller skates, and the cast have to be able to dance, skate and dance on skates in time to the music whilst singing the challenging yet beautiful melodies of Andrew Lloyd Webber. It's no small feat. When we first started the show back in 1984, I thought what are we doing? And yet bit by bit, everything came together and now the show is not only on tour around the world, but has also just celebrated it's 25th year in Bochum, Germany, where the show has it's own purpose built theatre.

Many judges seem to play up to a particular persona or allow the pressure of audience opinion and ratings sway their judgement, whereas you maintained professional throughout your time on *Strictly* and *So You Think You Can Dance?*. You are partly expected to be entertaining and partly expected to give a serious appraisal of dance performances. How did you approach your role on these programmes?

My role on any judging programme is always to be honest and direct. Of course on *Strictly* I used a lot of visual images to convey my point which the audience found funny, I recently bumped into Kate Garraway who told me I commented she was about a sexy as a brazil nut! As a choreographer I'm very demanding of my dancers, and I was equally the same with the celebrities on the show.

One of the advantages and pitfalls of exposure on television is increased press attention. How have you gone about managing your media profile?

I've been through many peaks and troughs with my media profile, first starting way back with Hot Gossip incurring the wrath of Mary Whitehouse. I've had some wonderful support over the years, especially since my departure from *Strictly*, however I've always been wary of the press, for just as one minute they love you, the next they don't.

You are known for being extremely hard-working, are you are workaholic or do you think you have achieved a good work/life balance?

I will tell you I think I have a very healthy work/life balance, my family however will disagree and are always telling me to slow down. After just turning

70, most people would think I'd at least be thinking about it, but as far as I'm concerned I'll be dancing into my 100's.

You have come a very long way since your first interests in dance as a child to West End and then television acclaim. How do you account for your success?

I put my success down to passion, determination, drive and the amazing support of my family. My focus and energy keep going, and having had my children late in life definitely keeps me young.

What would be your advice to someone who wants to work in the entertainment industry?

My advice to someone who wants to work in the industry is always have a back up. Negative as it might seem, it is a world of rejection, and that's before you've even opened your mouth, or stepped on a stage. As famous or talented as you might be, it could literally come down to being the wrong height. Saying that, if it really is the only thing you have ever wanted or are going to do, you need an unwavering determination, and a passion like no other.

Sir Bruce Forsyth CBE

Entertainer, TV host

"Be absolutely natural, walk on a stage the same way you are meeting someone in the street for the first time, or at a party, just be absolutely yourself".

He has entertained American troops during WWII, prime time television audiences in the 1980s and students at Glastonbury. During a career that has spanned more than 70 years, successive generations have grown up with Sir Bruce at the heart of British television. The length of Sir Bruce's career is well documented, less well-known is the story behind his rise to prominence in the 1940s and 50s. Sir Bruce had no contacts and very little in the way of funding when he started performing dance routines in theatres around the country. To practice his acts he would have to tear up his parent's carpets so he could use their floorboards and the pay from his first professional act didn't even cover his transport home. He played second fiddle to major stage acts for 16 years before he hit the "big time" at the London Palladium in 1958. By the mid-Sixties Sir Bruce was the best paid entertainer on British television.

During the 1970s and 80s, Sir Bruce was a permanent fixture on British evening TV, presenting The Generation Game, Play Your Cards Right, The Price is Right and You Bet! After a period of relative obscurity, Sir Bruce's career was rejuvenated in 2003 following an appearance on the topical quiz show, Have I Got News For You?. "Nice to see you, to see you nice" was voted the most popular catchphrase in the UK in 2007. In 2013, the Guinness World Records recognised him as the "male TV entertainer with the longest career".

Thinking back to when you were just starting out, as Boy Bruce the Mighty Atom, what did you have to do to get yourself noticed as a young performer in the 1940s and 50s?

I started doing amateur shows during the war because my mother and father ran a variety company and in those days we could leave school at 14, so I left at 14 and went into show business. Back then you looked in The Stage or The Performer, which were theatrical magazines with work listings and you would get work through them. My first ever professional date was at the Theatre Royal in Bilston, which in those days was in an area called the Black Country because of all the mines. It was a dreadful show really, I mean really awful, but the producers managed to persuade my parents to put £25 into the kitty so we could all go ahead with this awful show. At the end of the week, we got paid depending on how big our billing was and I got paid in old money, 13 and fourpence for the week. I had to wire home to my mother and father to give me money for the train home which cost 35 shillings, and on top of that, I had to pay another 30 shillings for my digs, which would be about 65p today.

It's a million miles away from where you ended up.

Exactly, and my mother and father said to me, "do you still want to be in show business?" and I said "oh yes I'm going to love travelling to different towns and doing different shows". My main ambition in those days, and it was the ambition of every variety artist, was to work the number one theatres in the country, which were the Moss Empires. They were a top circuit of theatres and after that there was the Stole circuit, and then B. J. Butterworth's Butterworth theatres and then you had the real rat holes where you didn't even have a stage door-keeper, those were the dregs of theatre in this country. So there was first rate, second rate, third rate and fourth rate and I worked them all!!

You also managed to do a number of different acts during this early period.

I was a song-and-danceman and I played in a number of double acts. With the American Red Cross I did another double act which was a wonderful job to do – we both played the piano accordion, my partner was a great drummer and of course I sang and tap-danced, entertaining American troops in the run up to D-Day. When the Red Cross finished I went back to trying to get into variety theatres. You kept going, you had many weeks out but then you had many weeks in. Then I did a stint where I was in Jack Jackson's stage band and when that broke up they went to the number two theatres. Then I went to the Windmill Theatre and became a juvenile lead, a song-and-dance man again.

Did you ever contemplate packing it in?

Oh yes I certainly did! After I first went to the Windmill I got my calling up papers so I had to go into the RAF for two and a half years, after which I came back and did another stint at the Windmill and met my then wife, Penny Calvert. We tried getting jobs everywhere but finding a job as a dancing-singing act was difficult, you were either a dancing act or a singing act, you couldn't be both. We even went to India in an attempt to break out as a song-and-dance couple. We worked in a hotel in Karachi and a few others on the coast of India. When I came back I started wanting to do a single act and that was a big challenge because I didn't quite know how that would be accepted. I did quite well at that but I was always what they called "second spot comic" which means it was your job to go on after the dancing act. You had to try to warm the audience up which was a thankless job and I did it for three or four years and I did say that if I had to do that for the rest of my life in show business I would get out but just before the five years was up I got the job at the Palladium which changed everything.

The particular path you took to stardom, working the variety circuit for 16 years, is rare among most of today's top television performers. Do you think that has given you characteristics or ideals that have helped you during your television career?

Yes, I took me 16 years from the age of 14 to when I was 30, when I got the job at the London Palladium, that was the biggest job you could get in the country. I never begrudged those 16 years because I learnt so much in that time. Because it had taken such a long time, I appreciated it, whereas today, somebody can become a big star overnight and that is much more difficult to deal with. I wouldn't like that to have happened to me, I would rather have had all the experience I had than be suddenly thrown into another world that I knew nothing about.

Thinking about the experience of being on stage, you've talked about the highs from being on stage and performing to a large crowd, most recently at Glastonbury, but also at live performances in general. A lot of comedians in particular talk about having highs on stage but then they are often accompanied by quite severe lows off stage. Do you experience those highs and lows?

Yes show business is all about being high one minute and low the next. Even before that 16 years was up I would go to auditions and I wouldn't know whether they liked me or not and you never heard back. It was all part of the build up of getting somewhere in the business. You mentioned Glastonbury, that was the last thing in the world I thought I would ever do and the Albert Hall is that last place I thought I would ever appear. If it had been a disaster I could have said "it was a venue too far" and at my age you can make a big mistake and no one will think anything of it so long as you are honest! Glastonbury was the biggest reception I have ever received in my 70 years in show business, I have never had such a reception, with people chanting "Brucie! Brucie! Brucie!" before I even went on. What frightened me was so many young people there, it was an audience of people in their 20s, 30s and 40s, hardly any 50s or 60s, certainly no old people like me. It was a young, young crowd, the people who criticise me in the newspapers for being old hat, using old material should have been there. If an audience of that age group can accept me then how can I be old hat? I am not a stand-up comedian, I'm an all-round entertainer. I sing, I dance, I play the piano, I do impressions and involve the audience for over two hours. It might not be stand-up but it doesn't mean it's dated.

A lot of your performances are ad-lib, particularly on Strictly and the like, within that, would you say there is a Sir Bruce formula to speak of?

Yes in my one man show there is a lot of places where it's ad-lib as well. I get four people out of the audience and have fun with them which is a 15-minute bit. That's all ad-lib because I don't know who I'm going to get, or what I'm going to say to them.

You are well known for having a series of mental exercises such as your Tibetan stretches, and some of the other techniques you use for keeping fit and getting in the right frame of mind. How did you come across these rituals and how do they help you?

I start in bed by doing different stretches and that takes me 10-15 minutes and then I get up and I do all my exercises, I do a lot of stretches and semi-yoga things. The trouble with me is I hear about a different exercise and I put it into my routine so the way I am going on I could be doing all these exercises until lunchtime and not even have breakfast! They have stood me in good stead and I finish by doing 25 twirls on the spot, twirling almost like a ballet dancer. If anybody normally tries to do that even four times they would fall flat on their face but I do it 25 times and I finish up steady as a rock. It's supposed to be very good for the metabolism and it certainly helps you wake up.

Are you are creature of habit in other aspects of your life?

Yes, I'm a very habitual person. I have a diet of sorts, although it's not a very strict diet, I do the hay diet where you don't eat potatoes, rice or bread with a meal. John Mills was a great man for that and he said a couple of times that he thought it saved his life. I do love potatoes on a Sunday but otherwise I keep all potatoes off my meals, it will be fish and meat with vegetables. I drink a lot of water, I have some fruit every day, so it's all the things that people have been telling us to do for years but who does them? I don't think anyone does them other than me.

You began at home, tearing up the carpet so you could dance on your parent's floorboards, and now you're one of Britain's best loved performers and that has also come with a dramatic improvement in

your living standards to put it one way. When you reflect, as you must do, on your career and the journey you have been on, what sort of things come to mind?

What has been so wonderful about my career is that I have been on primetime television now for 54 years, that's going back to the Palladium in 1958, up to Strictly in 2013. Every decade has more-or-less grown up with me, every ten years a new set of young children have grown up with me over that 70 years and they're still doing that. Children of 5, 6, 7 are growing up with Strictly and old granddad Bruce is on the TV on a Saturday night so that has been very gratifying. But I also consider myself to be very lucky that in all that time I have done the kind of shows that a family audience has enjoyed watching and that has just mounted up over the years. When I went to Glastonbury I was thinking "all these people who are 20 or 30 years old were seeing me 20 years ago when they were little children". That's something I am very grateful for.

How do you account for your own success?

Something I learnt very early on when I started doing a single act is to be yourself. Be absolutely natural, walk on a stage the same way you are meeting someone in the street for the first time, or at a party, just be absolutely yourself. When anybody writes me letters asking for advice in show business it's always the best advice I can give: be yourself, don't try to be anybody else. When I first started in the business doing a single act a great big impresario said to my agent "he talks too high, his voice should be lower, and he should talk in a pseudo-American accent". Sounding American was the flavour of the year. Big American comedians came to the Palladium and they were so good that people tried to copy them and talk in a pseudo-American voice. My agent told me to get a tape recorder and practice, and I tried and I thought, "how can I do this? This isn't me, I just want to be me". I did a week at the Empress Brixton, which was one of the largest variety theatres in London at the time, it was built like a cinema so it had a very cold atmosphere and it was very, very difficult to work there. I did a week there and I broke my heart because it was so bad and the reaction was so awful, I died every performance, I was so embarrassed I wouldn't even get a cup of tea in the green room. I stayed in my dressing room from when I got there to when I left it was so awful. The week after I did a week in -a very intimate old-fashioned theatre, the City Varieties, Leeds. I did exactly the same act as I'd done the week before and it went over wonderfully, but that's show business.

Chris Edwards

Co-founder and co-managing director, Poundworld

"In another interview I did the other day he asked "what drives you?" and I said it's the fear of going skint. People think what drives you is you are greedy and you want more money, it's the opposite, it's the fear of failure".

Chris started out working on his parents' market stall in West Yorkshire but today his retail chain has over 200 stores and achieved sales in excess of £200 million in 2012. In that year, the company opened 52 new outlets and plans to continue expanding at a similar rate. Despite being more than comfortable today, Chris still gets up at 7.30 every morning to go into work, often getting back after 19.00. He claims to be driven in part by his competitive nature and wanting to expand the business as well as the fear of failure. Like Poundland and 99p Stores, Poundworld's USP is providing all its goods for under £1. It's major difference, largely unique amongst similarly sized retail outlets, is that it is a family business, Chris' brother, Laurie, co-manages the firm and Chris' son is also involved in the business.

Chris puts the success of Poundworld down to its simple offering - "Everything £1" - as well as the family-run ethos of the company and the benefits of operating a value retailer during a recession. He started out in 1975 with one shop, rented for £100 per week, but feels they failed to capitalise on the economic downturns in the 80s and 90s due to lack of experience. In 1982, Chris bought an old Mecca shop and started up a nightclub. He had to borrow heavily from his close family to get the business off the ground and the experience has left him with an aversion to debt, something that has served him well since the 2008 financial crisis. Whereas other major retailers became overwhelmed by the debts they built up during the growth period, Poundworld has largely financed its own, explosive, growth.

You have gone from working on a market stall to running a nationwide business – many shop owners start with plans to expand massively but find themselves falling short – why do you think Poundworld has been successful where other retail ventures haven't?

I think there's two things there, working from the market to where we are now, that was never pre-planned, we always planned to have some shops but never to be nationwide. The reason why we are successful at the minute is two things; value for money always makes you successful and the recession has added to that. So whereas it took us to get from one to one hundred shops over many years, we've gone from one hundred shops to two hundred shops in two years. That's because the recession has affected us in several ways, it's helped that there has been a lack of money in people's pockets, so they are buying for value. The second thing is that landlords took a hit with major retailers going down so there are many more opportunities on the high street and incentives to get you on the high street.

So is there anything about your particular approach that you think has been instrumental for Poundworld's success?

No I think our approach is very, very, basic. We've improved our offering in the actual stores and the standard of the shops but otherwise no. The longer you go on for and the quicker you're expanding, from a landlord's point of view, it gives you a better covenant. It's not just one factor, it's many factors, financially, you can do it quicker because you are not having to borrow so much money because you are getting incentives from landlords and there is more opportunity to become a stronger covenant from a landlord's point of view, so the better the covenant you are, the better the offer you get when you want to open in their stores.

What sort of experiences do you think have helped you from your time on the stall?

It is just evolution, you don't realise how much experience you are gaining, you're just keen to get there. It's like many things, I remember negotiating for the first shop we had, and that goes back to 1975, and it was a local property, I can never forget, I think at that time I was offered, rental rates combined £100 a week. It has been a learning process, for example, during the recession in the 80s, we weren't experienced enough to take advantage of what was going on on the high street, but when the next major recession hit, which is the one we're in now, the experience then had accumulated to a point where we knew how to maximise what was going on around us.

It's about learning a lot over a long period.

Yes it's about always learning, you say "what given thing" but when I first started buying, I used to buy from wholesalers in Leeds and Manchester, and that's as far as we went. Now we have a Hong Kong office and a Shanghai office and again, it's just evolution, we opened the Hong Kong office about ten years ago and that led to the Shanghai office, for different reasons to the Hong Kong office, three or four years ago.

So you didn't start with a long term strategy for nationwide growth?

We have a long term strategy now, we've had a long term strategy for eight years, but prior to that, which is the bulk of my experience, it was just the opposite, you just played it as it comes, on a daily, let alone a weekly basis.

That's interesting, I had assumed you had a plan for "taking over the world", or at least the country, from much earlier on.

No, no, I go into many corporate meetings and people ask me the question about where my motivation comes from and I say: "well my motivation was, going back to 1970-something, just to feed my children".

But that was enough of a drive to push Poundworld in the direction it has taken.

That's the only driver, no aspirations of taking on the world, just to have a handful of shops in Scotland was enough for me, let alone an office in Shanghai and Hong Kong.

Now that you have enough to feed your family, and probably quite a few, what drives you now, now that getting by isn't as much of a factor?

From my point of view, my son has just come into the business, he's 30 now and he came in when he was 16. He's very much a strong driving force, to support him, is one major thing, and you get the sense of achievement and the challenge, you've got the competitive nature there. They always say in business you've got to get something out of it for yourself, rather than just looking at it financially. I think you've got to get a sense of satisfaction from it all.

So it's the satisfaction of seeing it grow and develop and become something you are proud of.

It's about the people you work with and from my point-of-view, it keeps me alive, I mean mentally.

You've talked about the responsibility of having 4000 staff working for you and working 24/7 to keep the operation going. Do you have to stick to a rigid timetable to get all your work done? What is your

daily routine like?

Very much so, yes, I get into the office between 7.00 and 7.30 every day, it varies a bit, but it's mainly between 7.00 and 7.30 and I rarely leave the office until 18.30 or 19.30, so it's long hours. When you're motivated and you're driving forward, a day in here, for some people sat behind a desk it may seem like an eternity, but for me every day is like 10 minutes.

So within that time frame, are you a creature of habit?

No, play it as it comes, anything can happen and we'll deal with it accordingly. There's no set lunch breaks or whatever, it's just play it as it comes.

Very much the ethos you started with.

That's right, in my job I don't even have a PA, my son goes crazy, and I say "you can't teach an old dog new tricks!".

Does he badger you a lot about things like that?

Every day.

Really?

Every minute of every day.

People have talked about Poundworld having a "family ethos", why do you think that is the case, have you set out to create that sort of feel?

I think it's that typical self-employed attitude of "if we're going to win, we're going to win on our own merit because nobody's going to give us anything". You just work as hard as you can every day.

It seems to have worked.

It might sound condescending but it's not, that's how it is, it's built in. There's just messages every day, now especially, with what's going on in the high street, thinking about Peacocks, Woolworths and Comet. In another interview I did the other day he asked "what drives you?" and I said it's the fear of going skint. People think what drives you is you are greedy and you want more money, it's the opposite, it's the fear of failure.

Looking at those particular retailers you mentioned, what would be your advice to major shop owners in the current climate? Or to someone starting out.

My advice is you need a good offering that speaks for itself, that's the first thing. I've looked at and I've analysed Comet and Peacocks in particular, and I've noticed the difference between being a soultrader to the corporate position we have now moved to. I've noticed corporates could, five years ago borrow a lot, whereas we have kept our borrowing down deliberately. When I've seen the level of borrowed money they've got, and it was a ridiculous amount of money, and you just think "they can't work", I mean, it probably would have worked if the recession hadn't kicked in. They hadn't made the precaution of defending themselves in the event of a downturn, the borrowed money exposes you. So I think the chains of shops have exposed themselves to too much borrowed money and when the banks want to pull back, they can't cope with it.

Is that the major failure you think has taken place there?

Yes, I think it's the borrowed money and the bank's involvement. I was just reading about the demise of Jessops and the realisation that once the bank moves in and says "we need to reduce our commitment to you", it can't be dealt with, because if the sales are down in the stores, and behind the scenes they are squeezing to lower your loan or deed commitment, they just over borrowed, they just can't deal with it. From our point-of-view, we have the same bank facility as we had when we had 100 shops.

Sticking to borrowing, and going back to your earlier period, were there any big risks you felt you took to bring about growth?

Yes, without a doubt, at the beginning, the first bit of borrowed money I took on our first store was so little and we had that under control but when we had half a dozen shops I moved on and opened some nightclubs. I once bought a nightclub for, at the time, in 1982, an agreed a price of £360,000 and my bank refused to lend me the money. The guy who was selling it introduced me to his bank and I managed to do the deal but the outcome of that deal was that I had to put my house on the line, for security, I had to put my brother's house on the line, and my father's house on the line. I went to each one of them and I said "I can't borrow the money" and both of them obviously offered me the benefit and I took it. Now if somebody said for the same deal would I do that again, the answer would be no, I think I did it because I was naive, fortunately it was a successful business operation, I realise now with everything else I have done that it could have failed as much as it succeeded.

You now have 208 stores in the country, what are your plans for the future?

If everything stays the same, we are now on course for opening 50 stores per year for the next two or three years. So we are trying to keep the positives going, it would be naive to say we are on a roll and nothing can fail, because it can. If it remains, much of a muchness, where it has been for the last couple of years then we can maintain the 50 stores per year opening programme.

What would you say is different about Poundworld when compared to 99p Stores or Poundland?

This is all very much of a muchness to a point, it's your quirks, Poundland is owned by a major company, and I do know the originator of Poundland, I remember when he started because we had several meetings at different times in the Far East and he has been to see us up here in the last 12 months but he sold up many years ago, as you are probably aware. VC sold twice, so it's very much corporate and they've got unlimited funding, but we think we can match them with experience if not with funding. So with Poundland, that's a big corporate animal and it's doing very well and they are well run and I wouldn't knock them in the slightest. With 99p Stores, they're very much similar to us, but their culture is very different to us, you will have seen that on the programme about us recently on the TV. I think we're different, I think we set a better standard, and they probably think they set a better standard, but the offering is much of a muchness.

Is there anything you would do differently, looking back on your career?

I think I would have started on this expansion a bit earlier if the opportunity had been there. That's the only thing I would do differently, maybe buying from the Far East a little sooner.

Catherine Johnson

Writer and screenwriter, *Mamma Mia!*

"My agent called me and told me this idea was going around and we both laughed, you know, "it's a new musical about the ABBA hits", we both thought the idea was extraordinarily funny".

The success of *Mamma Mia!* has come as something of a surprise to its writer, Catherine Johnson, who expected to be returning to write *Byker Grove* scripts shortly after meeting ABBA composers Benny Andersson and Byjön Ulvaeus. As the show opened in the West End, Catherine was busy looking for the next job, not believing the musical would make very much money. But the production she thought would last three months ended up lasting more than ten years, making it the 10th longest running Broadway musical, grossing over \$2 billion worldwide and is now the highest grossing musical film of all time.

With the success of the show, Johnson was given her due for an all-consuming addiction to writing that began when she was just 6-years-old. Whilst at her Gloucestershire primary school, Catherine "was very well behaved and very keen and eager to please" but as secondary education dragged on, she grew bored of academia, and also found she increasingly needed more time to herself, taking time off lessons to be alone, have a cigarette or read a book. Johnson's improvised timetable caused a great deal of friction between her and the school, who asked her to leave after a clash with the headmaster. Expelled at the age of 16, Johnson now tried to work for Debenhams in Bristol but found her continuing need for solitude got in the way of her job.

She balanced a number of part-time roles whilst writing radio plays and looking after her children. In 1987 a play-writing competition ran by HTV and the Bristol Old Vic caught her eye and she began work on her first play-script. By now Johnson was at the stage where she was seriously considering joining a college and getting qualifications if her writing career did not start to support her. She already had her first child, Hugh, and was expecting another, Myfi. Her first play, 'Rag Doll', won the competition and was shown at the Bristol Old Vic. Her reputation improved considerably, but more importantly, she felt she had, at last, found her "calling".

When did you first discover your interest in writing?

Right at the beginning when I was about six-years-old and we were asked to put forward pieces for a competition. It was the putting together of words, the forming of the story, it just excited me, it's the feeling of control I suppose. That was the point when I really felt I wanted to be a writer of some sort but it took me an awfully long to think, "ah, it's scripts, that's what I should be writing!"

So did you close off to other things at that stage, was it definitely writing?

No, I had fancies for other things along the way, because I loved going to the theatre, I thought about acting but that wasn't a very serious thought, I don't have that level of confidence and I never thought about directing. I guess it was as if "I will always write", somehow, somewhere, but I didn't always think it would be a career, it would just be the thing I do because it was so natural to me…

It was part of you, rather than a career.

Exactly, so I was interested in psychology for instance but I never thought of life without writing something down at some point every day.

Your school days were quite a difficult period for you and your teachers, were you always a rebellious child?

Not always, that came a bit later, I was very well behaved and I worked very hard when I was in primary school and I was very keen and eager to please. What went wrong? I still don't know. I got bored actually, I did start to wonder why I was doing these things that I was so not interested in doing and I also found I needed a certain amount of time each day by myself so I used to take a lot of time off lessons to sit by myself, have a cigarette, eat a sandwich. To me, it seemed OK, I thought I could get my energy back for the next lesson, get some focus. Extraordinarily, the school felt this wasn't on at all so we began to clash and I got worse as the clashes continued.

So what was the final straw then for the school?

The day I went in wearing a halterneck top and told the headmaster where to go, that was the final straw and that is when I was expelled and education ended for me at that moment.

You've talked about how when you were young you needed to spend time by yourself and that you never really considered any other career path. Did you feel dragged along by your writing at any point?

Yes, that's a really interesting question to ask because you are absolutely right, there were times where I used to wish I was doing something, anything, else because it doesn't ever stop. There isn't a moment where you go, "right that's it now." It's a compulsion and an addiction. I am really grateful that I have it too.

It's living other people's lives in your own head.

That's it, yes, I do feel like I don't live a whole life. I live a life of observation and a life of inner dialogue. I do very much need to be by myself as much as possible.

What was it like, initially, being asked to work with ABBA?

I laughed my head off. My agent called me and told me this idea was going around and the producer would like to meet me and we both laughed, you know, "it's a new musical about the ABBA hits", we both thought the idea was extraordinarily funny and said: "Yeah of course, just to tell people I had met ABBA, that's something isn't it? Even if I never get to do the work."

So you didn't think at that stage that it would even happen, because ABBA may not allow it to happen, or whether they would take you on?

I didn't know whether they would take me on. When I met the producer she told me the idea did have the backing of Benny and Byjön, but they were going to be very rigorous in overlooking the project and I needed to convince them with the right idea, the right storyline and they would work very closely with the whole production, once we got over that first hurdle of preparing the storyline. But after meeting them a few times I forgot really that they were ABBA and they just became the guys I worked with and still now there's that thing where I see them and it is great to see them but then you are put in a situation where you've got people going: "it's Benny, it's Byjön", and I think: "Of course they are famous as well, I forget!"

The main thing that the press like to say about you is that you went from rags to riches, and that was quite quick as well, it must have been around 1999-2000, when *Mamma Mia!* first came out.

I did go from being really quite hard up when I first started writing, even when I had won the competition, it was an extraordinary amount of money I felt at the time, it was £2000, but it wasn't an awful lot in the scheme of things. So I very quickly moved from theatre to television just to earn enough to tick over but by the time I got the job for *Mamma Mia!*, I had a house, I had a mortgage, I mean, it was tricky, it wasn't as bad as it had been, I still had to try to earn enough money to pay for everything, so I was always chasing the next commission, I was never comfortable enough to take a week off, or even a weekend off at that point.

I got the job for *Mamma Mia!* and for the two years working on that, really for no money because I got paid the original commission, it was a scary-ish time because I was always thinking, this is keeping me bobbing along but you can't afford for anything to go wrong because I can't pay for anything to go wrong. Really, nobody had expected *Mamma Mia!* to make any money so was thinking: this is going to open and three months later it will close, I need to be already in the swing of the next project.

The plot of *Mamma Mia!* concerns itself partly with the life a single mother. Did you see yourself as Donna at all?

I did absolutely want to write about the single mother who wasn't a wretched kind of – you know – at that time there was a lot of press about single mothers being a drain on the state etc. so I wanted to write about a working single mother who had got her life together and the relationship she had with her daughter who she absolutely adored but fought with. So that part was very much based on my relationship with both my children. But the character I identified with far more is Donna's friend, Rosie, who's a writer and is a much more "I'll go my own way, I'll do my own thing" sort of character. That's the one I felt was most based on me.

You had no idea that it would become one of the highest grossing musicals ever?

No, the thought that it is over ten years and it's still running, it doesn't make sense somehow.

Did you give any thought to making it into a film, when you were working on the play?

Not right at the beginning. Judy, the producer, always had this at the back of her mind, that it was either going to be a play, or a film. She decided to make it a stage play before she met me so she was thinking about it well before the offers started coming in. Actually as soon as *Mamma Mia!* opened in America, the film studios started getting in touch so we knew from about the first year that one day it would be a movie. It was just a matter of holding our nerve and not selling the rights because it might have been quite tempting to accept an offer in that first year and then somebody else would have made the movie and then that would have been it. But Judy held on and held on and eventually said "right, we will work with you but I am not selling the rights to you".

So you wanted control, even at that point.

Yes and I think it's why *Mamma Mia!* has been successful, in a sense, is because all the people who have worked on the stage show have worked on the movie so it's very much kept the spirit intact.

Overall, are you now comfortable with *Mamma Mia!* being, for now, your masterwork? Do you get people bothering you about it, linking ABBA references into conversations?

Not so much people in general but there are very few journalists who can resist that and it always amusing me because I think: "In ten years do you think you are the first person that has done that?" No, I am absolutely happy for *Mamma Mia!* to be my life, my world, because I know there are other things I can do but I can't ignore the fact that *Mamma Mia!* is always going to be the biggest thing.

Chrissie Rucker MBE

Founder, The White Company

"From the moment the idea happened I believed so passionately that it could work".

During a refurbishment of her boyfriend's home Chrissie found it was impossible to find white home-wares in national retailers that were both affordable and good quality. After extensive market research she found that white bed linen, table covers, towels and china, were generally either poor quality and cheap or luxury items that were too expensive for the majority of consumers. Chrissie launched The White Company as a mail order business in 1993 with the aim of providing excellent quality white products at an affordable price. She left her job as a beauty journalist on *Harper's & Queen* and started to build the business from scratch.

20 years later, the company has evolved enormously, opening up its own retail stores and expanding its product range to include women's clothing and nightwear as well as a wide range of gifts, home accessories and furniture. The Little White Company was also launched in 1996, after the birth of Chrissie's first baby to offer children's bedding, clothes and nursery furniture. In 2012 Chrissie was awarded the PWC and Financial Times Private Businesswoman Of The Year Award, in 2013 The White Company had over 50 stores in the UK and an annual turnover of £120 million.

On the face of it, setting up a business that sells only white products seems like a bizarre business plan. What is the background to how that idea came about?

I often joke that really I was just trying to show Nick (who was then my boyfriend) what excellent wife material I was! I went off shopping to look for lovely white linen, towels, bathrobes, china and napkins for his new home – because I just love the aesthetics of these items in white. However when I arrived at the big department stores, I found it wasn't easy to find. At that time, there was a lot of colour and pattern and not a huge amount of white. The white I could find was either cheap, poor quality embroidered designs that looked like it might fall apart quite quickly, or big brand, fabulous quality with high thread counts and fine yarns that were very expensive. At the designer end I also found that the sales assistants were a bit snooty and some looked down their noses and directed me to the cheaper ranges in the store! So the shopping experience wasn't great either.

Shortly after this, we went to stay with Nick's sister Susie and she had just been through exactly the same thing, and then she said "wouldn't it be brilliant if there was a company that just sold white things?". So that was it, and I couldn't sleep for the next couple of weeks because I was so excited. I was a journalist, so I started to research. I rang a number of department stores and I spun them the yarn that I was doing a piece in the Sunday Times about 'white in homes' and I asked them what percentage of their bed linen sales were in white. The great news was they consistently said it was over 50%.

It was a convergence of my genuine love for all things white and then finding it really hard to find.   My mission therefore with The White Company was to offer first-class designer quality but at affordable, high street prices – 'affordable luxury', because it just wasn't there. Secondly I wanted my company to make everyone feel welcome, there would be no snooty sales assistance and we would be there to help and give great customer service.

One example that explains quite well what we do is that one of my first products was a beautiful bedspread made in Portugal. It had previously been sold by a big brand for the £250, back in the 90's. However we could retail the same bedspread, exactly the same quality for just £85. So that's really what is at the heart of the business, we source directly from some of the best factories in the world and we don't add high designer margins.

How did you feel about leaving *Harper's* & *Queen*?

I loved my time at *Harper's* and all the other magazines I had worked on before, but I wasn't a very good journalist! The great thing about working in that world is you learn how to put an article together. You also learn a lot about styling so it was a fantastic foundation of knowledge that I could then apply to the business. I started it as a mail-order business which in many ways is like putting together a little magazine so it was an invaluable experience to have had.

I was also mentally in a place where I was ready for a change. I remember getting off a plane after a holiday, Nick went back to work full of excitement and anticipation whereas I had more of a "going back to school" feeling. From the moment the idea happened I believed so passionately that it could work, so I just went off and made it happen. I am not a traditional business person, I have a C in maths O-Level! I didn't think about numbers, I just believed in the idea so much and thought "right I'm going to leave my job and give it a year, if it doesn't work I'll just get another job".

I was 24 when I started and I also did a short three day business course with an organisation called Centec which was the government scheme backing enterprise back then. They gave me a grant of £50 per week for 6 months, this paid for my food and I sold some shares that my grandmother had left me for £6,000 and I started the business with that.

Walking into a White Company shop is a great visual experience. What sort of effect do you hope to achieve? Do you have an idea of how someone is supposed to feel when they go into one of your shops?

We want it go be a great experience the minute you walk through the door. To be inspiring and exciting, inviting and welcoming, yet calm and serene. Some of our customers actually tell us they love it so much they often pop in just to calm down if they are having a bad day! We want it to be somewhere you love to spend time in, a bit like home really and somewhere you know you can trust the quality, advice and service.

When it comes to running the business, would you say you are an instinctual person when deciding the product range or the design of the shops, or are you more methodical?

I am definitely a very instinctive "from the gut" sort of person. My passion and strength is on the product side, I am hopeless at operations and structure! My real focus today is on looking after the brand and the overall brand experience we deliver for the customer.

Have you found it easy to delegate as the business has grown? Especially in a company that is so personal and very much something that is about your own passions.

Yes I have and I think it's because I am very aware of where I can add value and where I can't. Many years ago I also went on a delegation course, it was just a one day course, but it was transformational and it taught me how to hand things over. It's something you get better at with time and experience but I am a great believer in seeking advice and guidance from people who are experts in their field. I believe you are only ever as good as the team of people you have around you. In a fast growing business, it is crucial to have the right people in the right place at the right time.

Coming from a non-business background, what did the process of setting up and running the business teach you about business? Were there any significant surprises along the way?

As a business grows, it constantly presents different challenges. When I was young I used to ride competitively and with this you have days when it goes really well and you have days when it goes really badly! You tend to have more days of it going badly than really well, but you just get back on and have another go and try not make the same mistake again. I just tried to apply that to difficulties as they have come along in the business. I'm a great believer in never being afraid to ask for help, of course I was also very lucky to have my husband who had already started his business 3 years ahead of me. A lot of the teething problems he went through, I went through as well and I was very lucky to have that mentorship at home.

You mentioned your husband, Nick, did you have any other role models to speak of when you were starting your business?

Back then, Nick had started Charles Tyrwhitt and Johnnie Boden had started Boden so those were the two similar mail-order businesses I looked to. I admire hugely what Estée Lauder has achieved, she started life selling one lip stick and the business has gone on and become this fabulous global brand and still remained family run. I have never sold any shares in the company. Today I seek a lot of guidance from our Chairman Tony Campbell and my CEO Will Kernan. Plus I love talking and sharing with other business owners.

What personal qualities do you think you have needed to make the business a success?

It really depends on what sort of person you are and where you can most add value in your business. I am very focused on three things. One, keeping the brand vision clear and true. Two, doing everything we possibly can to give our customers a great experience. Three, building a brilliant team across the business and our supply base to make it all happen.

We also always have a clear vision and goal for the future, usually a five-year plan. I believe it's vital to constantly listen to our customers and our team to help make good decisions going forward. It's also really important to celebrate the good days and keep everyone smiling.

Christian Horner OBE

Team Principal, Infiniti Red Bull Racing

"When Red Bull first came into Formula One we played our music loud and had the reputation as a party team, perhaps not particularly serious, but behind that, yes we did play the music loud but there was a fierce determination, we knew what we wanted to achieve and what our aspirations were and still are".

For the man that has lead Red Bull Racing to consecutive Drivers' and Constructors' Championship victories, it all started with a go-kart in his parents' back-garden. That early experience gave Christian an enthusiasm for speed that has never left him, leading to his first career as a race driver as well as a second career as a team manager. He was awarded the prestigious Renault Formula One scholarship in 1991 and finished as a race winner in the 1992 British Formula Renault Championship. Christian progressed to Formula Three and Formula Two and eventually to Formula 3000 level but remembers the moment he realised his racing days were numbered, "I remember coming out of the pit lane and seeing Pablo Montoya head into the first turn completely on the edge of adhesion with the car totally committed in a perfect four-wheel drift and I thought, "I can't do that"".

In 1997, Christian formed his own team, Arden International, which went on to win a string of victories within Formula 3000. Red Bull entered Formula One in 2005, having bought the unsuccessful Jaguar Racing team the year before. Christian was the youngest team principal in the business, having impressed Red Bull with the setting up and managing of his own team in Formula 3000. Being a Team Principal in Formula One is often confused with being a football manager, but as Christian points out in this interview, his role has more in common with that of a CEO, heading up an organisation of 550 people with operations across engineering, logistics, finance and marketing. Red Bull won the Constructors' and Drivers' Championships in 2010, 2011 and 2012.

What was your childhood like?

I had a very happy childhood, I'm in the middle of three brothers and I grew up in the countryside. I had a fascination with speed from a very early age, whether it was making a wooden go-kart to go down a hill or a moped to ride around the garden on. From a very early age I was fascinated by speed and then I discovered the world of kart-racing.

At what stage did that become competitive?

I remember for my twelfth birthday I managed to persuade my mother, because I knew my father would never agree, to buy an old beat-up go-kart and the idea was to drive it around the garden. We found it in the local newspaper and it was actually a 20-year-old racing kart, hopelessly beat-up and it was too low to go around the garden. So we went up to a local track at Shenington, at the top of Edgehill and I discovered the world of kart-racing. Then for my next birthday got a proper kart that I could race with.

How did school fit into all that?

My older brother was quite academic and I went to a good prep school in Leamington Spa called Arnold Lodge and then Warwick's Boy School. I made some good friends there but school was almost a bit of a social thing for me in as much as my mind was always somewhere else. When I started racing it was at weekends and so on and I managed to combine it quite well with school until I was about 16 years of age, then it started to get a bit more competitive as I started to race overseas and I needed to take the odd day out here and there.

Was it difficult achieving a balance because you were obviously prioritising racing quite heavily? Were you not slightly jeopardising your education at that stage?

It was a balance and my parents were always very clear that I had to complete my education. I was very keen to leave school at 17 as the racing was starting to go okay but my parents insisted that I stayed and completed my A-Levels and be able to go to university which I had absolutely zero intention of doing but I managed to complete my studies and felt as if I had upheld that part of the deal.

Jumping ahead quite a bit, how did you make the transition from racing to management?

It was by accident. I had started my own team because of the demand of finance, which is the way it is in motorsport. Car racing is expensive and I had worked very hard to raise sponsorship and rather than go to a poor team and see that hard-earned money spent unwisely, I felt the most cost-effective thing to do was to buy a car and take on a couple of guys within the team. I employed two part-time mechanics at that time and ran the car myself and I thought at least at the end of the year I would have a car, rather than just some pictures and a pair of overalls. It was a means to an end initially but I was racing against some very talented guys like Pablo Montoya and Tom Christiansen, and I was honest with myself that the higher I went in motorsport the harder it got. I was okay but there were lots of drivers that were okay and very few elite ones. I had grown up in the sport, I was passionate about the sport, I had been good at generating funding to fund my own career and suddenly I had built this little team and I thought, "well okay, if I stopped I could create a career in motorsport just not behind the steering wheel".

In terms of the actual timing how did you know when specifically to make that move?

At the beginning of the 1998 season I remember doing a test and coming out of the pit lane and seeing Pablo Montoya head into the first turn completely on the edge of adhesion with the car totally committed in a perfect four-wheel drift and I thought: "I can't do that". There is a barrier just on the outside of that turn and I was honest, I knew then, and that was before the season had even started, so the beginning of '98, I knew that was going to be my last year.

What needed to be done to turn Red Bull into the high-performing team that it is now?

The first thing was to understand what talent was here and how the team operated, so I spent the first three months just looking and listening and learning and applying the instincts that had served me well within my own team. Formula One, like any business, is a people business and you have got to have the right people in the right area. What was obvious to me was there were a lot of talented people here but it lacked technical direction and clear focus and vision. There had been a revolving door in the Jaguar days of different management structures that had been and gone. It was then a question of identifying who the right guy was going to be to move the engineering team forward. I was a big fan of Adrian Newey from watching the cars that he had created with Nigel Mansell and Damon Hill. For me he was the best guy in the business, there were people at the time who were saying he had had his time but I really wanted him in our team and set about persuading him to join us as well as recruiting other key positions in different areas of the team and team management, the chief designer, the head of aerodynamics, we gradually collected a very talented group of people.

Was it difficult to pull it up by its shoestrings so to speak?

When Red Bull first came into Formula One we played our music loud and had the reputation as a party team, perhaps not particularly serious but behind that, yes we did play the music loud but there was a fierce determination, we knew what we wanted to achieve and what our aspirations were and still are. Again, you see a lot more people here wearing jeans and t-shirts than perhaps in some of our more corporate rivals and I think we've got a great team spirit here.

So that Red Bull ethos runs through the team.

Yes it was important to incorporate that and still at the same time be totally professional and focused on what the end goal is and bit-by-bit people bought into that, especially when you bring in a guy like Adrian Newey.

Is it helpful to have a fun-loving atmosphere within a team?

Yes, it's hard work and it's hard pressure so it's important to have that balance between all-out drive for what you are trying to achieve and creating an environment that people enjoying working in as well.

Coming back to the race itself, that is an extremely high pressure and emotional environment, how do you deal with that very intense period, you always seem fairly calm on TV.

I try to be, the race is only one element of the role that I do, but it is obviously a very important role and I just try to address things objectively, panic has never won a Grand Prix. Everybody should know what their roles are, it's something we practice for and a calm head in high pressure moments is extremely important.

How would you characterise your management style?

I never had any formal training in management but I believe the best form of management is about getting the best out of people and recruiting the right people and backing them rather than telling them how to do their job. A lot of what I do is ensuring people are clear on what their targets and objectives are and clearing any obstacles so that they can perform at their best and I think it is important to be accessible and to be open and bring the best out of people.

Your role is often compared to being like a football manager whereas in reality you are managing a whole business as well as managing individual races.

You're running a business as well as running a team, you're a football manager for 20 Sundays a year and then you're a CEO for the other 250 days of the year. This is a business of 550 people and the sporting element is a key element but it is an element of what the business is and you have got to have that balance.

What would you say are the major challenges that face the Team Principal of a Formula One team that did not exist 10, or 15 years ago?

I think commercially the stakes are much higher. The amount of money that is involved in the sport, the politics, as money becomes more involved politics becomes more prevalent. The advancement of technologies as well is something that has had a big impact on performance.

What advice would you give to someone who would like a career in sports management in general?

I think you've got to trust your instinct, there's all sorts of people who would be happy to give advice and opinions but you've got to trust your instinct. I think that fundamentally sport management, or business management, it's about understanding people and being inward looking as well as outward looking. You need to think about how are you going to get the best out of those individuals and get them to work as a team, rather than as individuals.

David Abraham

CEO, Channel 4

"At the sharp end of the creative process is this fascination with what makes an original idea, whether it's music, or the written word, or fashion, if that is your guiding light, then honing that skill and developing it is one of the most critical factors that creates value".

The son of two immigrants, his mother was from Belgium and his father was from Calcutta, David Abraham grew up in rural Lincolnshire and Essex and went on to study History at Magdalen College, Oxford. Amazingly, David's application to study television at postgraduate level was turned down by Middlesex Polytechnic and he started a career in advertising after a friend suggested the industry might also provide him with the opportunity to be involved in creative work.

David co-founded the groundbreaking advertising agency, St. Luke's, which continues to work with major clients today. He moved out of advertising in 2001, becoming General Manager for Discovery in Europe and later joined UKTV as its Chief Executive. He is well known for having initiated the successful rebranding of the UKTV channels that saw the creation of the Dave, Alibi and Yesterday TV brands. David describes his career as having taken place in a series of roughly five to seven year periods, giving him time to learn and make a positive impact in each role. His advice is to stay in a role for long enough to have made a measurable achievement before moving onto the next challenge.

Channel 4's distinctive ethos is in part due to the fact that, like the BBC, it is legally required to offer the public a strict balance of current affairs, factual and entertainment formats as well as investing in innovative homegrown content. But unlike the BBC, it has to pay its own way. When he joined Channel 4 in 2010, the organisation was seen to be at a bit of a creative ebb, with Big Brother having dominated its schedule for years, to the point where it seemed to define the channel itself. David has led the rejuvenation of the channel post Big Brother, returning it to its core values, overseeing the development of new programmes and the growth of Channel 4's on-demand service, 4oD.

You began your career in advertising; did you always see that as a route to working within television?

To be honest, I had some pretty general aspirations of wanting to be in the creative business. I think that is partly because of my background, my father was an architect who worked in designing schools and homes in the public sector but most of my family were entrepreneurs or involved in business. As I was growing up I probably was exposed to the balance between creativity and business in a very general sense. Then at university a lot of my friends were heading into very pure business and finance and I always wanted to find my way into the creative world, but I think I decided very early on that I wasn't a performer, a writer or a director. Being a producer of those things interested me more.

I did actually apply straight out of university, after studying History, to do a postgraduate course in TV production at Middlesex. It was in the days when there were very few graduate-level jobs. The BBC had a few traineeships, but if you didn't get one of those it was all a bit ad-hoc. There was a small course in television production, funnily enough I didn't get a place there but a friend of mine said, "ad agencies produce a lot of content and are partly in that world, why don't you go and look at that?" Once I understood how that would work I realised it would fulfill that side of what I was looking for because it was to do with thinking about brands and often communicating through film, imagery and writing. Many of the creative people in advertising are the sort of people who are also doing other things as well, sometimes on the side or maybe go on to do other things. I probably stayed in the business for longer than I thought I would but I always felt I was always going to go back to a purer creative environment rather than the commercial art of advertising.

Do you feel that you probably did a lot more on the creative side having been in advertising, rather than doing production which puts more of an emphasis on the logistical side of things?

Possibly, I mean, it's difficult to imagine how things might have worked out differently. I was lucky that I always worked in very creative ad agencies like CDP and Chiat/Day. There are companies which are more commercially driven but I was always at the end of the market that was trying to innovate and do interesting things. Advertising is really focused on ideas and I learnt about the process of generating ideas, collaborating in teams, how you use consumer research to shape ideas but still keep them original. They are quite good at training people to be good managers as well, the big agencies were in my day, in the eighties, and so you came out with quite a few good business skills as well such as numeracy and the mechanics of marketing. If you put those things together it was a good training ground. At the same time, when I left advertising in 2001 I went into a reasonably senior role at Discovery and had a very steep learning curve to understand the disciplines of broadcasting as opposed to just a minor or general understanding of how television works.

When you left advertising and moved to Discovery, what were your aims? Did the company have a specific idea of what they wanted you to do when they hired you?

I came to it in part because this was the stage when independent companies were being spawned and I came to look at it as a sector that was interesting and different. Just by chance I got approached to run Discovery in Europe and I took a decision that this would be a really exciting new point in my career. I think what they were looking for was someone to grow their channels and get them to connect with audiences on a bigger platform, because obviously in the early days of multi-channel television, pre-digital, they were very niche channels that many people were not exposed to. But with the growth of multi-channel they knew they could reach more people so my background in advertising and marketing was very relevant. We developed a digital portfolio of channels at Discovery and we grew the business and did quite a few interesting deals with our partners and I got to commission programmes that won some awards. All of that was a great four years' experience for me and then I got asked by the American arm of Discovery to help them run their learning channel, TLC, over there which I did for nearly three years and that was a whole other experience, transposing everything into an American environment was very exciting.

The creative sector seems to be quite an unpredictable career path, you talked about your friends from university going into straight finance or business areas and you wouldn't expect the kind of movement that you've had. I guess you wouldn't have predicted how much you have moved into different areas?

I think I've worked in different settings but there's been continuity from where I was at the beginning to where I am now. The consistency has been helping to manage creative teams in environments that are highly committed to innovation Chiat/Day the advertising agency I worked at prior to St. Luke's was a very innovative American company and has been throughout the last thirty years, creating the Apple brand. I have always been drawn to that but, yes; things have worked on a sort of five to seven year cycle in terms of where I've done it. I think the balancing act in terms of managing your career in the media is to make sure you establish a body of work before you feel the need to move on to the next thing because the opposite of that is you don't stay long enough to really make an impact.

Turning to your present role as CEO of Channel 4, what does that position involve, in a very broad sense?

Ultimately I have to set the vision of the organisation in terms of how it's responding to the changes that are going on, so that we don't become isolated and obviously with technology things are changing very rapidly at the moment and positioning us within that context is key. I've got to set a culture and build a team that can deliver to the innovation agenda, particularly with regards to programmes we commission but also the way in which we deliver them to the audience from a production and technology point-of-view. I'm responsible for the revenue of the organisation. Although we are publicly owned at Channel 4, we are independently funded through our advertising activities so I have a revenue line I am managing with 200 people in our advertising department and they are turning over £1 billion in revenue these days. So it has a core to it which is a conventional CEO job but I have this public remit which requires us to deliver more than that. We aim to deliver programming which has public value, whether it's News and Current Affairs, which other channels under-invest in, or whether it's programming that is particularly giving opportunities to people who are at the beginning of their creative careers, in writing or performance or technicians. So we have within our remit, which we are held accountable to by Parliament and by Ofcom, a specific set of ambitions that we have to be accountable to.

Channel 4 is restricted to a set of public service requirements much in the way the BBC is with its Charter. I wanted to ask you about a specific part of the Communications Act which is the need for Channel 4 to "exhibit a distinctive character", how do you think this manifests itself in practice?

It's got to be innovative and risk-taking and you've got to try new things. You can only really demonstrate this through specific examples so if you were to take the Paralympic Games from last year, they hadn't been broadcasted in that way or at that scale with that kind of impact so that is a very good recent example. Then in specific areas like film, we are supporters of many different independent filmmakers over many decades that have gone on to do great things that are also part of our remit. The News and Current Affairs output, you've got a whole hour of in-depth news every day at seven, that's an example of something which we probably wouldn't do if we were a purely commercial broadcaster. There are many quite famous and popular characters in British broadcasting that began their careers at Channel 4, whether it's Graham Norton or Jonathan Ross or dramatists like Shane

Meadows and Paul Abbott who have done their first work with us because of our appetite to back emerging talent. We're sometimes described as the R&D lab of British television and I quite like that description although of course the environment we are doing that in now is much more cramped than it was thirty years ago when we were set up. We don't have a monopoly over innovation but it certainly demonstrates by our very existence that we are a balance to the BBC, who of course receive all their funding from the license fee and we provide direct competition to them which is probably a good thing given their scale.

You started at Channel 4 at a time when it seemed to be at a bit of a creative ebb, what were your priorities when you joined?

There were a number of things going on at that point, one of which was informed by a debate around our funding and whether we should try to get direct public funding of some kind. Our new chairman and I set out our stall so as to remain independent and not get public funding which meant we had to run the place as efficiently as we possibly could and create new partnerships and find new revenue. In addition to that, Big Brother had been on the schedules for a decade and we probably got a bit over-reliant on it. It had created an image of our brand which was dominated by one programme so the push has been on making the schedule much more diverse and making a lot more programmes and working with more producers to make those programmes in order to re-diversify the schedule. The observation sometimes comes from our commercial competitors that we should have a Coronation Street or an X Factor in order to compete with them but we hope we are trying to do something different here. I think we have over forty new shows on our schedule every year which is a far healthier place to be in my view.

On-demand sources for entertainment are proving increasingly popular, particularly for the under 30s, how do you think that attitudinal change is going to effect the funding model for Channel 4 over the next ten years?

It's already beginning to affect us in as much as we have 4oD which is a rapidly growing platform to catch-up with Channel 4 content and we have now got YouView which is emerging as a new way in which Freeview and broadband can work together amongst the main public service broadcasters. All of this is starting to generate new opportunities for engaging directly with audiences. We announced eighteen months ago that we are going to develop our own relationship platform so that we can have a closer dialogue with the viewers in a way that we have never been able to do before. What's been encouraging is that over seven million people as of this point in the year have registered with Channel 4 and for the first time they are able to receive messages from us and personalise their experience of 4oD. All of these things are creating data which, blended with the needs of advertisers, can create more value around the audiences.

You've worked across different areas of the creative industries throughout your career with a close eye on the commercial side as well as the production of content, what would be your advice to someone who is interested in a role within the creative industries?

I think the most important thing is to be passionate about ideas and finding new ways of saying what might already be familiar in order to get people to see things in new ways. If you are passionate about original ideas, it will stand you in very good stead in whatever environment you may find yourself in. Obviously there are many, many jobs in the Media that are to do with the commercial side, the legal side, the technical side and these are all very important functions. It's very interesting for example if you come from a legal background to do a legal role within a media organisation. So there are lots of specialist roles that form part of the whole but at the sharp end of the creative process is this fascination with what makes an original idea, whether it's music, or the written word, or fashion, if that is your guiding light, then honing that skill and developing it is one of the most critical factors that really creates value. I think that is the greatest ambition that people should really think about because if they want to work at a more operational level that's great too but you would want to work to do that in a creative environment rather than just anywhere. We don't produce a product mechanically; it is literally the ideas that come out of people's heads that create value

Donato Coco

Director of Design, Lotus Cars

"My first decision was to cancel the tea room - not very popular in England – and turn it into a virtual room with big screen to visualise projects with optimal conditions".

Donato Coco's obsession with automotive design began while he was in his school years, copying out sketches of the cars that he found most inspiring. His career really began when Citroen spotted the young designer's talents in a competition and sponsored him through the Royal College of Art where he received a Masters in Automotive Design.

Prior to working at Lotus, Donato Coco rose to become Chief Designer at Citroen, heading up the design teams that produced the Xsara, C3 and Picasso amongst others. More recently he worked on the Ferrari F458, F430 and California as Ferrari's Director of Design and Development. His role at Lotus has perhaps been his most challenging yet, tasked with producing six new concepts in ten months as part of the company's efforts to demonstrate its new focus on innovation and bolster its drive to up production of its light-weight sports cars. This lead to a dramatic overhaul of the company's style department that included a controversial decision to replace the department's tea room with an advanced design studio and put a greater emphasis on style in a company that had long been directed by engineering interests.

You showed an interest in car design at a very early age, even drawing sketches of Lotus cars during your childhood, how did you approach getting into the world of car design?

In the beginning you learn by just observing and reproducing. One day I discovered Giorgetto Giugiaro's Lotus Esprit S1 sketch and I was so fascinated by this beautiful black-and-white ink side view of what became a mythical Lotus car, that I reproduced it 100 times before I was able to draw it identically.

Later, when I was 24, I was designing ski goggles and helmets for a French company near Geneva when I found in a magazine a National Design Contest organised by Automobile Citroen. While I was furiously drawing my design proposal at home, I ran out of colour markers and had to send the sketches unfinished with a letter of apology. Six weeks later I received in return a letter saying that they did not understand why I had sent my proposal one month earlier than the deadline but they were happy to announce to me that not only I was the winner of the contest but that Citroen design director Carl Olsen wanted to meet me at their headquarters.

I was hired by Citroen and sent to the Royal College of Art in London to prepare a Masters in Automotive Design. When I came back to Paris I really started my career with Citroen where I grew and learnt on the job, followed by Ferrari where I continued to learn about sports cars, and now I am at Lotus trying to reinvent the brand. This was the way I approached getting into the world of car design.

How do you go about formulating a new design from scratch, especially with a brand like Lotus or Ferrari where the design needs to relate to a motoring history that goes back many decades?

These brands of great notoriety like Lotus and Ferrari have their roots encored in motor racing and so far have logically created commercial products that are consistent with this long racing tradition and philosophy. Before formulating a new design, it is important to look at the history and understand the brand values, having in mind the soul of the company founders such as Enzo Ferrari or Colin Chapman, characterised by the absolute obsession for innovation; "the next car, the one that still need to be invented is the important one". Innovation is essential but looking back to history does not necessarily give the solution for the innovations to come, you still have to invent them and be coherent with tradition.

When you joined Lotus in 2009 the company was initiating a huge sales drive, with an aim to bring in ten months six new concepts to illustrate the rebirth of Lotus at the Paris Motor Show, what did you have to do to get Lotus up to speed when you arrived?

When I joined Lotus I found a styling studio unequipped and empty of important projects, a team small and talented but not used to defending styling interest in this company traditionally driven by engineers. It was imperative to find a new balance and start to nurture a company-wide design-led culture to deliver desirable products with higher perceived quality. I had to re-orientate the styling studio from a small, mostly consultancy focused operation into a world class OEM facility.

My first decision was to cancel the tea room - not very popular in England – and turn it into a virtual room with big screen to visualise projects with optimal conditions. I rapidly grew the team of designers and modelers from seventeen to seventy to be able to deliver this phenomenal plan to bring six new concepts to Paris Motor Show 2010.

What is a normal day like for you and how much of it is direct design work?

There is no normality, each day is full of surprises, except starting the day by writing my plan on a white page of paper. To design requires time for imagining and projecting ideas and also the time to realise them physically. Everything is related to design work and my mind is permanently connected to the ongoing design process on projects, wherever I am.

To make the styling dream come through I also need to dedicate time for planning, budget, meetings and negotiations, all necessary activities to support, to defend and to promote the design ideas, but I am very much attentive and close to the daily design work. I dedicate the maximum time to it, giving design directions, reviewing sketches, CAS models, 3D models, because it is where each day you make the final difference.

What skills do you think someone needs to be a great car designer?

A car is a complex product and the designer has an essential role to unify functions within synthesis shapes that must also deliver strong-unique personalities, coherent with the brand values. The designer needs artistic skills but must also have taste and interest for the technique. The finality of the car designer action being a three-dimensional object he has to understand and practice sculpture. Technical design skills like sketching, creating computer imagery and surfaces are needed and the designer can learn them.

What skills to be a great car designer? Skills don't make it all, more fundamental capacities are needed: "imagination", "sense of proportions", "sense of harmony" and a fitting spirit with a bit of poetry, which have more to do with your genes than with what you can learn in a school.ten text here. Insert chapter ten text here. Insert chapter ten text here. Insert chapter ten text here. Insert chapter ten text here. Insert chapter ten text here. Insert chapter ten text here. Insert chapter ten text here. Insert chapter ten text here. Insert chapter ten text here. Insert chapter ten text here. Insert chapter ten text here. Insert chapter ten text here. Insert chapter ten text here. Insert chapter ten text here.

Evan Davis

Economist and journalist
Presenter, BBC Radio 4 *Today* and *The Bottom Line*. BBC 2 *Dragons' Den*.

"By studying economics and understanding economics more I had an outlook on the world that was, you can call it narrow, you can call it overly mechanistic, but it was an outlook on the world, we want our journalists to have an outlook on the world".

Evan Davis has taken an unconventional path into journalism, becoming an established economist before joining the BBC as a correspondent in the 1990s. Like many of the country's prominent figures from politics and journalism, he studied Politics, Philosophy and Economics at Oxford, gaining a First, and later undertook postgraduate studies at Harvard.

Following a period as an economics correspondent for BBC News and economics editor of *Newsnight*, he became the BBC's Economics Editor in 2001, making him the most senior economics reporter in the corporation. Today he is best known for presenting the BBC's reality business show, *Dragons' Den* and hosting the *Today* programme on Radio 4, alongside veteran broadcaster John Humphrys. Broadcasting since 1957, the *Today* programme attracts seven million listeners during its 06.00 to 09.00 weekday slot.

Evan has a knack for breaking down and explaining complex issues in business and economics in a way that can be easily understood by the average viewer, perhaps best demonstrated in his broadcasts for BBC News as well as the *Evanomics* blog series. He describes his work life today as being a "portfolio career", working on ad-hoc projects such as books, documentaries and live events alongside his radio and television commitments.

It's interesting that you started in economics, rather than journalism per se, what was the route you took to get where you are now, very broadly?

I think I had a better route into journalism than a lot of other people follow, in that there were two phases. Phase one was doing something non-journalistic, in my case, economics, working in the nether regions of academia really at the Institute of Fiscal Studies and the London Business School in fairly junior roles and immersing myself in it for quite a long time. I was studying economics beyond undergraduate level till I was aged 30 then I switched over and went into journalism, which was at the BBC. I think the best thing to say about it is that by spending those first ten years in phase one, I was in a much stronger position in phase two, I think I had a little expertise of my own.

You were able to differentiate yourself.

It was like a little rock on which I could stand in the messy world of journalism and people trying to establish themselves and it just gave me a base from which to pursue that career so I think it was a really good way of doing it which is why I always say to people who ask how they get a job I say, do something else first, get interested in something substantive, it just helps a lot. I should say also that the big thing is that by studying economics and understanding economics more I had an outlook on the world that was, you can call it narrow, you can call it overly mechanistic, but it was an outlook on the world. We want our journalists to have an outlook on the world, I'd like some religious people in journalism, I'd like some biologists and scientists in journalism, I'd like some economists, historians, there are lots of outlooks on the world you can have but it would be very nice to think that they have one. It's good if they can come with something, that they bring something to the party, rather than, they've left college studying, let's say English, gone on to study at journalism college and then gone straight to journalism where they haven't really had time to find their passion.

I guess it's kind of like the argument for people not having political careers, you do something else first.

It is a similar argument, that it makes you a better politician if you've gone out a bit and I think there is something in that, but I'm arguing really both that you are a better journalist for it and it's also a helpful way to get on if you come at it with something.

How much have you been able to indulge your really quite academic understanding of economics within a career in broadcasting?

My view is I think my academic understanding of economics has not been used on a daily basis, obviously, with what we put out on radio and TV, but I do think that what goes out is very well informed by it. It is very helpful if you want to simplify things and explain, it is very helpful to have an understanding beyond that which you need to get across. I basically see myself as a simplifier, as someone who boils things down and I try to do that quite intelligently, keeping the essence of things, while nevertheless making it very simple and I think it is very helpful that I know more about the subject than would be apparent in what I say. I think you have to be reasonably advanced to do a good simplification job, basically.

Your work day is extremely unusual compared to most peoples as I believe you have to get up at 3.15 in the morning, and the Today Show finishes at 9.00, how do you organise your work life?

My work life is very organised and very controlled because the one thing professionals tend to have is lives where there are very few boundaries between work and home life and work hours can spread and there is no kind of formality or rota, clocking on or clocking off. What's great about the *Today* programme is it really is very regimented, I've got all my work days timetabled and I know exactly which days I'm doing, which makes it a lot easier to control my life around that than if I was in some other role. Even when I was Economics Editor, it was quite a pain because I didn't know which night of the week I would be working, I didn't know when I would be on the 10 o'clock news, which just made life difficult to manage. The *Today* programme has a few formal hours, you've got two or three days of that, getting in at 3.45-4.00, leaving at 9.30-10.00 and then I've got a few days a year on *Dragons' Den*, quite a few days a year at The Bottom Line and around that I just do projects and other things. I do some public speaking, hosting of events, quite a lot of chairing, I'm writing a book at the moment so that is something I have to fit in within the other hours so basically life becomes a lot more project orientated, rather than work-day orientated and the regiment of the *Today* programme makes that possible. It's like a sort-of portfolio career, that you are able to do a little bit of this and a little bit of that and fit it around your main job.

So is it difficult to discipline something that could potentially be quite all-over-the-place?

Well I'm very easily distracted so I am not very good at self-discipline, I am very good at doing things that have to be done, like lots of other people, so the writing side is the slowest because I am very slow at writing. I am very easily distracted so I might be reading something relevant to what I am writing and then I find myself reading something else, it's all useful, but it is all very ill-disciplined, I'm not a sort-of, "I'm going to do 1800 words today and here they are" kind of person.

You regularly interview important figures from business, politics and the media. When it comes to interview technique, you are known for being more relaxed and less aggressive than some of your colleagues. Do you think your style has an advantage over more heavy-handed interviewers? Can you draw out more from a less aggressive

approach?

I think there are merits to there being lots of different approaches so my contention on this is that you don't just want there to be one kind of style, or default style of interview or discourse. I think occasionally it has been seen at the BBC that there is a style of interview that is convivial and kind of light-weight and that forensic means aggressive. I think that has occasionally been seen to be the case but I don't see that as the case. We ought to have different types of interview, even within the *Today* programme there doesn't have to be one style, we should hold people to account, that is one of our roles but it's not our only role. There's this rather pompous journalistic phrase, "speaking the truth to power" and that is one role of journalism. I just think that a lot of different styles is good.

I don't think I get more out of people, some people say, "oh you get more out of people because you're friendly and they lower their guard", I don't think that's true, I think they maintain their guard anyway if I'm honest. To be absolutely honest, I don't think I could be John Humphrys even if I wanted to be John Humphrys so I make no effort whatsoever to be like John Humphrys. If you go on the radio or television you can't be anything other than who you are and what you have to do is just pray to God that what you are is liked by enough people that you can carry on in employment. If people don't like who you are they are sure not to like who are when you are trying to be something that you aren't. It's an interesting topic though whether the adversarial interview is good or bad and I have come to the conclusion that it's neither good nor bad. We just don't want it to be the only show in town.

You draw out different things.

I'll tell you where I think adversarial interviews are unfair is when politicians have difficult decisions to make. I think sometimes it can sound like you are blaming them for the fact that they have to make a difficult decision. We live in a second-best world and you need to be careful about that.

This book is focused on how individuals have been successful in different areas, you are exposed to some of the top entrepreneurial minds in the country through both *Dragons' Den* and the *The Bottom Line*, what are the most interesting characteristics you have noticed from meeting some of these people?

On the entrepreneurial side, which is different to the business side, remember entrepreneurs are a subset of business people and they are different, for example, from your average chief executive of a large company, so you don't want to confuse those two. The real difference is that entrepreneurs just go on and get things done rather than talk about doing them, they just get out of bed and instead of thinking about things they actually do them and that is a really important characteristic and a fascinating characteristic really because most of us don't, most of us, we think about it but then we put it aside, having thought about it so that kind of "make it happen" philosophy is most important. I'm not sure you can force yourself to be like that, you can probably nurture it but I'm not sure if you can create it from nothing.

So that's number one, going alongside that is a kind of innate optimism, and maybe it's the optimism that drives them to do stuff, they perhaps think that what they are going to do on a given day is going to have more of an effect than most of us do. On the general business side, there are so many different types of people in business, so many different characteristics, so many strengths, so many weaknesses. All forms of life exist in business and I don't know what sort of generalisations I would make from senior executives, they are a much less interesting breed than entrepreneurs by and large, they are a much more wary breed than entrepreneurs too. Careers in business have elements of luck about them, the place where you work, right place at the right time, in general in careers there's no doubt that attitude is the most important thing rather than aptitude.

Dragons' Den has been praised for raising the profile of entrepreneurialism in the UK, as well as being criticised for presenting quite a distorted view of the work that normally goes into securing a £100,000 investment, what do you hope aspirational people take away from the programme?

I hope people don't take away that that's how the venture capital industry really works because it's an entertainment programme, so it's not going to be exactly equivalent to the conditions facing small businesses. I've learnt a lot from *Dragons' Den*, what sorts of questions are the right sorts of questions to ask and why is what you get from that programme. So I think it has had quite a big educational effect, first with the sort of propositions that come into the public mind via that programme and after ten series I am actually quite proud to think that it has helped and people really do think it has had an effect, people tell me it has had an effect in schools and in the mindset of younger people in particular. I think you do observe what makes a successful or an unsuccessful product and what kinds of questions you would ask and it puts the whole idea of an entrepreneurial career on the map.

I remember when I went to school, which was some years ago now, those little entrepreneurial neurones were not firing in most of us, it just wasn't really something that you thought about, so it's great that at least that little piece of the brain has been awoken in a lot of people by the programme and I think that is a very positive thing. It's not that I think everybody should be entrepreneurs, and I have never believed in saying to people "oh just try, try, try again, live your dream and persevere", most people shouldn't persevere, they're not cut out for it, they are never going to make it so we don't want everyone to be entrepreneurs but it's nice that that little piece has been awoken for people and have begun to pick up some of the knowledge and the language of the area. For everybody else it is very entertaining and it helps to understand the entrepreneur's predicament a little better too. So I think it is good for entrepreneurs and non-entrepreneurs, just to introduce people to a little vocabulary and what discourse might consist of. Of course you can criticise it for not being realistic but I don't find any of those criticisms get to the point, the point is it's a television programme with elements of reality about it, major elements of reality about it, and those elements are very interesting and very educational.

Geoffrey Howe CH, QC
(Lord Howe of Aberavon)

Chancellor of the Exchequer 1979-83, Foreign Secretary 1983-89

"I said to him, we need to do this as if we are running as a relay team and we have to hand over the baton, Hong Kong is the baton and we must be careful not to drop it".

Margaret Thatcher's longest serving cabinet minister is well-known for the resignation speech many cite as having prompted her downfall but the majority of his ministerial career bears the hallmarks of a constructive working relationship that Howe characterises as having been "like a marriage". He first worked with Thatcher while she was Secretary of State for Education under Ted Heath and attributes the longevity of their careers to shared ideals and a mutual appreciation of the other's abilities. Howe became Chancellor of Exchequer during a time of extreme economic uncertainty in Britain, overseeing the radical 1981 Budget that some credit with having brought Britain out of the gloom of the 1970s and cementing the monetarist policies that remained central to successive Budgets thereafter.

Lord Howe contested the seat for his hometown of Port Talbot twice before being successfully elected to Parliament. Prior to that, he served in the Royal Signal Corps, conducting operations in East Africa. On his first day at Cambridge, the representative of the university's Conservative Association knocked on his door and successfully recruited him to the Conservative Party "not because of strong political commitment but because of an interest in taking part in politics". Lord Howe's advice to anyone interested in a career in politics is to find a fall-back profession first, in his case law, which he took up after leaving Cambridge.

How great a role did politics play in your childhood?

I became interested in politics partly through my friendship with a school friend called Robert Sheaf. We decided that he was going to go into the Navy and I was going to go into politics and he did go into the Navy and then he became a Liberal. We were both interested in the school debating society and also in history and politics which was almost inevitable given that I witnessed the German bombing in 1940. I enlisted in the Home Guard and enjoyed that and it became clear that I was going to need to be in the Army and enlisted fully in

1944. Also the whole framework of studying Greek and Latin history stimulated an interest in politics. My father was a lawyer, he himself was never involved as a political activist but he was intensely interested in what I was interested in.

To go from school to Army to Kenya put you in a situation where you became more aware of political issues. Then whilst training for the Royal Signals I was based in Exeter with colleagues from all over the country. We had a Scot from Glasgow and Jackie from Falmouth and I shared a room with a man from Cardiff. It gave a very comprehensive appraisal of the country. Jackie from Falmouth and I were in Trafalgar Square on VE Day. I heard Churchill speak there and I saw Churchill driving through Trafalgar Square. We both went to Cambridge after we had been through the Army, he went on to become a geography teacher and wrote geography textbooks. When we met in London for VE Day we were treated like soldiers because we were in our uniform, and enjoyed all of that enormously. He wrote a letter to his parents, which I have quoted in my book, in his PS to his parents he wrote "Geoffrey is quite a decent guy, even though he is a public school boy".

This awareness of politics was something that translated into a more active interest at Cambridge.

On my first day at Cambridge I had the Conservative Association college representative knocking on my door asking if I would like to join the Conservative Party to which I said yes, not because of strong political commitment but because of an interest in taking part in politics.

You've described your relationship with Thatcher as being like a marriage, how did that marriage manifest itself on a practical level?

We were more-or-less contemporaries, although she was at Oxford, I was at Cambridge, we came to meet in the Conservative Lawyers Association. At the time we were in the shadow cabinet together we were asked to work together by Ted Heath. We were often asked to cool down Keith Joseph as well as working together on the legal side of the education system. At my 80th birthday, Margaret was there and people noted that she was and I reminded them that we had worked together for 18 years and that they ought to concentrate on the marriage rather than the divorce.

So until the tail-end I guess working with her was quite pleasant.

It was yes, to some extent quite often we were critical of Francis Pym who was a more left-wing figure on certain issues and Jim Prior who was more on the right, we made it a bit more balanced, certainly on economic policy. Another

other interesting thing about Margaret, incidentally, when you looked at the people at her 80th birthday, was the tremendous number of international figures that turned up. She was able to have a worldwide appeal, by being the first woman Prime Minister. Going with her to a Tokyo summit, seeing her speaking as one of the heads of government at a Japanese press conference, it was packed with Japanese women who had come to see this female phenomenon.

It must have been like being around a superstar?

Yes but not always like working with a superstar.

You were Margaret Thatcher's longest serving cabinet minister, why do you think you were able to stay in government while others came and went?

Because we had known each other, and indeed we had worked together, for common objectives for such a long time. I think that we found ourselves day-to-day close to each other, from the first time we met. We found ourselves obliged to work together on the legal side of the education system. I was advising Thatcher, as Secretary of State for Education so it became quite natural for us to be working alongside each other. The European objective became the most common objective in all our time together. We were working towards liberalising Europe, and defending and promoting Britain's interests - and were very much together in that. But I was surprised, on one occasion when I went to see her in 1990 – It was then that I was moved from Foreign Secretary to being Leader of the House. But fortunately that did work well.

What was it in the end that tipped the balance for you and led to your resignation?

My anxiety that she wasn't considering the European issue seriously. "No, no, no" was her refrain, I didn't feel that I was going to bring her down or anything like that, it wasn't designed to achieve that. I felt I couldn't go on wearing two hats. It is not easy now to recall or define the cause or causes of our falling apart. Simply growth of several differences in our analysis or prediction - and agreed perception that was indeed adrift. But, as I began my resignation letter on 1st November 1990, I said, "I do so with very great regret…It has been a privilege and an honour for me to have contributed to that success".

The upcoming transition of Hong Kong was something you had to deal with as Foreign Secretary. What was your experience of dealing with the Chinese during this period?

It was fascinating, and surprisingly so, because they were so comprehensive and forthcoming, Deng Xiaoping was really the figure who was the leader during the crucial period. I remember he said to me that he knew Hong Kong would continue to be successful because the American government had told him that American companies would continue to invest in Hong Kong and he could rely on that. I said, "well the British already invest in Hong Kong but people don't invest in places because they are told to, they invest because it attracts them and it is a good place that as it is" and I said that it's a magnet. His understanding of that was completely comprehensive, he had been in France in the 1930s and he was very responsive and intelligent and so were his successors, I found them completely candid and comprehensive. They loved metaphors, just as I used the magnetic metaphor, we were doing all this at the time of the Los Angeles Olympics and I said to him, "we need to see this as if we are running as a relay team and we have to hand over the baton, Hong Kong is the baton and we must be careful not to drop it". So that kind of dialogue went very well.

That explains how it went so smoothly, to an extent.

Yes we recognised that we had objectives and so did other people. The Queen on her state visit there, on her return banquet at lunchtime, she was sitting opposite Deng Xiaoping, I was sitting next to him and he was looking slightly restless before we started eating and she said, "I think Mr Deng looks like he needs a cigarette, could you tell him so from me?", and I did and he didn't, it was like a dog with two tails. It was a very good demonstration of intelligent people working towards objectives.

What advice would you give to someone who is interested in a career in politics and government?

Well that they should foster and enjoy it but above all to establish a career not dependent on politics, they need to have financial independence.

So securing a profession.

Yes but by all means they can do them at the same time, but you do need that, because I did, I was thrown out in 1966, and immediately I was back to my practice. I've always said that you need an independent existence, that's a negative aspect but it also gives you a positive input you can make, I was able to make that through the legal work I had done, the work I did with the Bow Group and of course my African experience with the Royal Signals.

Gerard Baker

Editor-in-Chief, Dow Jones & Co. Managing Editor, the *Wall Street Journal*

"When I went to New York in 1986, I just completely fell in love with the place and I became determined to go and live in the city".

On the night of 18th June 1970, when most eight-year-olds were fast asleep, the young Gerard Baker was wide awake watching the live results of that year's general election in the UK. He was, in his own words, "a bit of an odd creature in that respect", with an advanced interest in and understanding of history, politics and current affairs. Born and raised in Britain, a combination of intellectual curiosity and a drive to be the best at school meant that Gerry secured a position to study Politics, Philosophy and Economics at Oxford, where he developed his fascination with markets and finance. Thinking the best outlet for his interests would be banking, his first jobs after university were working as an economic analyst at the Bank of England and Lloyds.

Like much of his generation of students, Gerry lent towards the left of the political spectrum at Oxford. It was a time when the ideals of socialism remained widely popular and the advantages and disadvantages of the two competing political systems were still widely debated. He was elected as a Labour vice-president of his students' union and graduated with First-Class Honours in 1986. Any enthusiasm for socialism was quickly eradicated when Gerry took a trip to the Soviet Union, followed shortly by another to New York, which for him confirmed the merits of Western capitalism and further encouraged his lifelong interest in American politics and culture

The *Wall Street Journal* is America's best-selling newspaper with a daily circulation of more than two million copies. It was established in 1889 when the founders of Dow Jones & Co, Charles Dow and Edward Jones, converted the *Customers' Afternoon Letter* into an independent source of financial information for New Yorkers. After News Corp took over Dow Jones in 2007, the *Journal* has done something very rare in the recent history of newspapers in the West, it has increased circulation. Lead by its new editor, Robert Thomson, the *Journal* diversified into in-depth coverage of politics, foreign affairs, arts and sports, all the while maintaining a broadly impartial and intelligent tone that has made it one of the most trusted news sources in the world. Whilst most major newspapers both in the UK and the US have experienced a sharp decline in print circulation over the last ten years, the *Journal* has held onto its core readership whilst expanding into new areas. Despite its success, Gerry is not complacent about the decline of print media and spends most of his time working on the WSJ's many digital outlets.

Gerry worked at the BBC from 1988 and 1993, mostly as a producer. Between 1994 and 2004, he worked for the *Financial Times*, initially in its Tokyo bureau before moving to Washington as chief of the bureau. He served as the US editor and assistant editor of the *Times of London* before being appointed deputy editor of the *Journal* and the Dow Jones newswires in 2009. He took over as editor in January 2013.

You had a range of interests while you were growing up, how did you work out what you wanted to do?

When I was at university I didn't have a very strong idea of what I wanted to do, although I had a vague idea that I wanted to go into politics because I had been quite involved in student politics. From a ridiculously early age I remember being fascinated by modern history and the day-to-day unfolding of history, politicians and great events. I had no desire to go into investment banking or anything mainstream, I looked at the Bank of England because it was at the policy end of the financial system and I was fascinated with policy, partly as a result of studying Politics, Philosophy and Economics. I was there barely longer than a year, I hated the place to be honest, but what attracted me to it was that I would be analysing these great financial and economic events.

From there I went to Lloyds Bank where I was an economist analysing Latin America. I was looking for the intellectual reward that I got when analysing politics and economics at university so there was a logical step into journalism although I had never really seen it in advance. By my mid-twenties I was disillusioned with politics, I really didn't like working in the financial sector and I was casting around for something else to do. I saw an advertisement in the *Economist*, for a television company looking for someone with a background in politics and economics to be a researcher. I applied and got the job.

In the 2011 discussion you had at the Hoover Institute, while you were deputy editor of the *Journal*, you described yourself as having had a "Damascene revelation" when you visited the Soviet Union and the United States. Could you outline how your view of the world changed as you went through university and then coming out of it?

My views did change pretty radically, I was definitely on the left, although I was never a hard lefty. I was elected as a Labour vice-president of the student union and I had some fairly predictable left-of-centre student views. Over the ten years after I left university my view evolved steadily and a number of factors were responsible for that. Having opposed, and I would say, almost despised

Thatcher in 1979, there were a series of landmarks in her administration, from the miners' strike to deregulation that steadily changed my views about the shortcomings of markets and the advantages of government intervention. I had never been a communist, or even close, but like most of the European left, certainly the British left, I viewed myself as somewhere between American capitalism and Soviet communism. That's probably too strong, I wasn't strictly neutral in that I was aware of how flawed, and ultimately evil, certain aspects of Soviet communism were but I was one of many people who thought there were good things about communism and good things about capitalism and we shouldn't see things in black and white.

In 1986 I did one of those government organised tourist parties to Moscow and what was then Leningrad. I was only in the Soviet Union for a week, I wouldn't claim that I studied it in any great depth, but the most striking thing I remember was just the drab uniformity of the place. I grew up in London in the 1970s, and although it was a long way from being the great global metropolis it is now, there was still a certain amount of vibrancy and it was an exciting city to go to. Moscow and Leningrad were just these monolithically grey, dull, lifeless places. To cap that by going to New York three or four months later, with all its colour and diversity, whatever remaining doubts I might have had about the relative virtues of the capitalist system versus the communist system were removed.

Did you direct yourself towards living in the States after 1986?

I never imagined I would live in the States, even in my twenties, but when I went to New York in 1986, I just completely fell in love with the place and I became determined to go and live in the city. I joined the BBC in 1988 and very quickly found a way to apply for a job in New York and very fortunately got one. Living in New York confirmed everything I had thought on my first visit there, I had an amazing time and I knew then I wanted to live an extended part of my life there. I had been interested for a long time in American elections, I had a fascination with elections everywhere, but I remember following the 1980 election when Reagan was elected very closely. I love the way elections in a vibrant democracy give you an insight into the geography and culture of a country and I enjoyed following the 1988 election as well. When I joined the *Financial Times* in 1994 I told them, "look I really want to be in America" and they offered me the job in Tokyo but with a view to an American opportunity in the future.

Most of the major papers in the Western world have experienced a very sharp decline in print sales over the last decade, how has the *Wall Street Journal* been able to grow its following at a time when

most other papers are consigning themselves to quite marked decline in print?

I think there are a number of factors. Firstly I should say that credit is due to a number of other people, namely my predecessor, Robert Thomson as well as Rupert Murdoch. One important factor in our success is that a lot of people need to read the *Journal* because it provides detailed business information. So we have a solid base there which is certainly not invulnerable but there is a core that a lot of other newspapers don't have. The second factor is that when News Corp took over, and Robert Thomson gets all the credit for this, the aim was very much to hold onto that base but also to build out and become a broader newspaper with more politics, general news, arts, culture, lifestyle and sport without diminishing the business news.

Another development, which is related to those two points, is that the US market is evolving very rapidly away from the big city model towards national papers. Unlike the UK, where you have around 12 national papers, in the States you have the *New York Times, Washington Post, LA Times, Houston Chronicle, San Diego Tribune*, there are hundreds of them, each covering their own patch. What the digital revolution has done is really sweep away the rationale for that because no one needed to read the *Denver Post*'s Washington coverage because they could, frankly, read higher quality coverage from a more national organisation. I think what's happening is the US newspaper market is evolving into a much more European or Japanese market and we and the *New York Times* and some of the other bigger papers are evolving into national newspapers. So one of the reasons why we are doing well is the business is consolidating around the big papers and we're one of them.

What do you think is going to save news organisations in the long run? Is it assumed that there will have to be online subscriptions for the *Washington Post* or the *Wall Street Journal*, or is it more a case of waiting and seeing how the shift to digital pans out over the next decade?

We can see, looking at print numbers and the habits of younger people, that the digital opportunity is steadily eroding traditional modes of media. I think it is fair that we assume steady print decline, but I would say one cautionary word on that as it is still the case in the US that more than 50 million printed newspapers are sold every day. Even if that market shrinks at between five to eight per cent a year, that's still a lot of newspapers that are going to be sold and as big as we are, we are selling less than three per cent of newspapers sold in the United States. We could take more market share, even as the market declines, in the print field but an increasing amount of our efforts are devoted to working on the digital product and getting it right on its various models. It's odd because I find we talk about Wsj.com as the "traditional" platform, now that mobile and tablet outlets are becoming the growth areas. The medium-term aim for us is to maximise our digital subscriptions, maximise digital advertising revenue and find ways to expand profitably in the digital field.

How much of the business side of running the *Wall Street Journal* do you get involved in, versus the editorial side?

I spend a lot of time strategising over how to develop the many platforms that the *Journal* is now available on. On a day-to-day basis I'm looking at the online editions, the iPad edition, mobile edition, making sure we are doing the right stories, talking to my digital editors about what we are doing with social media, video and blogs. Part of my day is spent putting out a printed newspaper in the evening but most of my day, when you are not dealing with the rubbish that you have to deal with as the manager of a large organisation, I am thinking about digital content. Something we can struggle with as traditional journalists is the temptation simply to adapt traditional print journalism for the online side and that is a big danger. When you're doing digital content you really have to start *tabula rasa*, without any preconception about how things may look on paper.

It's an extraordinary journey from a dissatisfied economic analyst to a trainee journalist at the BBC all the way to editing America's most widely circulated newspaper. How do you account for your own success?

I think I have an intellectual capability, I'm no Stephen Hawking, but I can problem solve, work with numbers, articulate words and grasp complex problems. I think what is specific to me is from a really early age I have loved history, loved the news and loved watching the news. One of my earliest memories is staying up to watch the 1970 general election result, I was eight. I have an eight-year-old now who is very bright and switched on but would not dream of staying up to watch election results. I was quite an odd creature in that respect but I have just imbibed this stuff from a really early age. I just loved the news business and I think that has equipped me really well because I have just absorbed it.

I think another thing is, and I am sorry to engage in management pschyo-babble, but I am fairly driven and ambitious. Again from a really early age I wanted to be top of the class at school, and then at university, but I was also driven to get into positions of leadership. I was president of my JCR at college and then I was vice-president of the students' union so I think I was just one of those people, and I say this, I hope, in a self-aware way, who is driven and ambitious. I don't think I'm ruthless, I don't want you to get the wrong idea, I try to make sure that I have time to fulfill other responsibilities which social human beings should be doing.

Hayley Parsons OBE

Founder & CEO, Gocompare.com

"Once you've made the decision to do it, go for it and don't look back".

The mother of two from Wales left school with just six GCSEs but is now thought to be worth roughly £95 million according to the Sunday Times Rich List. Hayley quit her job at Confused.com in 2006 with a plan to set up her own, better, price comparison site. It was an ambition driven partly by a lifelong desire to work for herself and the belief that she could deliver improved results for customers through a more sophisticated site. Gocompare.com has achieved an extraordinary rate of growth, posting pre-tax profits of £34.7 million for 2012 and processing a quote every second. She has, in her own words: "done all right for a Welsh girl from the valleys, eh?"

Like many business startups, Gocompare.com had a few challenging years before the site began to take off, but as is the case with so many entrepreneurs, she never lost faith in the usefulness of the idea. However, unlike most of the entrepreneurs in this series, Hayley's bravery in starting her own company is all the more acute because she sacrificed a well-paid job at Confused.com to make it happen. She entered insurance straight after school and had amassed 14 years of experience climbing the corporate hierarchy at Admiral, the owners of Confused.com before she started Gocompare.com. The site received some major financial support from insurance entrepreneur Tom Duggan and a loan from Esure that helped to cover the costs of its early development. As for Gio Compario, the company's ubiquitous Welsh opera-singing advocate, Hayley "wanted something that people literally couldn't forget", and she certainly achieved that.

A lot of people comment on how you left school with six GCSEs, what did you make of school?

I was never really somebody that loved school in the traditional sense. It's not that I didn't like learning new things, it was more to do with the fact that I just really wanted to stand on my own two feet. I never really liked the institution of school and just felt that I could be accomplishing more outside of that environment. The education system today is completely different to the one I experienced in my school days. Young people are growing up with technology as a second nature and the education system has gone from an archaic chalk and blackboard lecture, to an interactive experience that I feel is helping young people develop key skills.

Did you know what you wanted to do when you were growing up?

Yes, but it wasn't what I'm doing today! Funnily enough, I wanted to be an interior designer when I was growing up. You never know, if things had turned out differently, today all the houses in the UK could be covered in animal print or I could've had my very own *Changing Rooms* show. Now that I've said that, it's probably best that I went down the insurance route.

What was the original inspiration for the Gocompare.com venture?

I was part of the team at Admiral that launched Confused. At the time, price comparison sites were a completely new idea, so my role was to convince insurers that comparison sites were the future of the industry – but as you can image, that was easier said than done! I spent many happy years at Admiral and worked with some fantastically talented people. But ultimately I became dissatisfied with the direction that the comparison site industry was going. Back then, sites were solely focused on price and didn't mention the features of the policy. This meant that customers might've been getting cheap quotes, but weren't offered much information on the policy and could've found that they were missing out on features that they wanted. I decided that I could either stay where I was, or I could start something new and make a difference. The result was Gocompare.com

Gocompare.com was the first comparison site to display the features of insurance policies, not just the price. It is entirely consumer-focused and has always set out to demystify insurance and help people find the right policy at the right price. The needs of our customers have underpinned everything that we have done, and are still the most important influence on our company. This belief has not only helped us get where we are today, but has also made us the only price comparison website invited to be a member of the British Insurance Brokers' Association (BIBA) thanks to our focus on transparency and customer care.

So it's 2006, you have left your job at Admiral and you are on your own with some investment money and a relatively small team behind you. How did you go about establishing yourself in the very competitive world of price comparison sites? What was the strategy in your first year?

The early days were certainly a challenge. Trying to build a recognisable brand from scratch isn't an easy feat, and I would be lying if I said that it wasn't daunting. Gocompare.com got its initial funding from Tom Duggan, an insurance industry veteran. Having worked my entire adult life in the insurance industry, I had built up good relationships with people like Tom, so acquiring the initial start-up funding wasn't too difficult. To begin with we sought out to grow the business organically, building up a customer base and slowly gaining a share of the market. It wasn't until we heard of Tesco's plans to enter the price comparison industry that we really decided to step up our game, as carrying on the way we were could have meant getting muscled out of the market. We knew if we wanted to seriously compete we needed to raise more capital. We were able to secure an additional loan from Esure to help fund the step-up. With this investment we were able to build a brand that could challenge with the previous market-leaders, and realise our goals of creating a company that would put the power back in the hands of the customer when it came to shopping around for insurance. Our competitors had to change the way they operated to catch up with us, which allowed Gocompare.com to springboard ahead.

You've spoken about how some of your friends described you as a "fruitcake" for attempting to start your own site, how did you avoid getting perturbed, or were you perturbed, by the dangers of going it alone?

What's important to remember is that I was never 'going it alone'. I'd convinced some of my closest (and most talented) friends to join me in starting Gocompare.com, so even though I did have some people calling me crazy for leaving a very secure and well paid job, I also had some amazing people supporting me. A big part of it was believing that Gocompare.com was going to be successful. There has never been a moment where I've doubted Gocomapre.com potential. That, and the support from very special friends and my incredible family, made sure that I was never perturbed from starting Gocompare.com.

Where did the idea for Gio Compario, your opera-singing advocate, come from?
Our initial adverts were great at educating the consumer about comparison sites. But what we really wanted was an advert that people couldn't forget, it had to be an advert that made people look at their insurance renewal letter and think 'Gocompare'! So, we met with a brilliant husband and wife advertising team, Sian Vickers and Chris Wilkins and told them that we wanted something that people literally couldn't forget, and that's exactly what they gave us.

You have also talked about enjoying being in a male dominated

industry. Have you faced any difficulties as a woman in business and, if so, how have you overcome them?

I think that some women become transfixed with the 'glass ceiling'. I've always thought that if you believe there is a glass ceiling, you'll spend your life on the floor looking up at it. Anybody can be successful in any industry as long as they work hard and are nosey and noisy enough. To succeed in business you need to be brave enough to ask the right questions and talk to the right people, it's the only way you can learn to be better at what you do. If you spend your time thinking about what's holding you back, then you'll never move forward – it's wasted energy. In my experience, gender has nothing to do with how talented somebody is at their job. At Gocompare.com we have a mix of both male and female staff and management. Everybody is there because of how hard they work and how good they are at their job; gender isn't even a consideration.

What would be your advice to anyone interested in starting their own online business?

If you're thinking of starting your own online business the most important thing you can do is research the market. The internet is a fantastic tool for identifying a target market and checking out the competition. Look for a group of people who are just screaming out for something new or better than what's currently out there and then look at how you can provide that. Can you satisfy the demand? Can you get a team of people together who can take on the job? If you need funding, can you raise it? If you can, then start to look at the practicalities of starting your business. Before you commit to anything, it's really important to look at what your worst case scenario would be. If, for whatever reason, your business doesn't work out the way you thought it might, what would be the consequences for you? For instance, If you're leaving a secure job there's a good chance that you've got a strong enough background and CV to get another job, so it's not too risky. Once you've made the decision to do it, go for it and don't look back.

John Sergeant

Journalist & broadcaster BBC Chief Political Correspondent 1992-2000 ITN
Political Editor 2000-2002

*"I think the mistake is to imagine that just because you have been to a war zone that makes
you brave. No, it probably makes you frightened, it makes you nervous afterwards".*

John worked hard at school and gained a place at Oxford University
where he read Politics, Philosophy and Economics. He developed a passion for
comedy first, appearing in a series of sketch shows with Alan Bennett as well as
writing many of his own scripts. During a gap year is Washington he was in the
crowd that witnessed Martin Luther King's "I have a dream" speech, an
experience that solidified his interest in politics and sharpened his ideas for his
future career. John's first job in journalism was at the *Liverpool Echo*, where he
worked for three years before joining the BBC. He has reported on the Vietnam
War, the Troubles in Northern Ireland and the opening sessions of the European
Parliament.

In 1990, John won the British Press Guild award for most memorable
broadcast after being shoved aside by Margaret Thatcher's press secretary, Sir
Bernard Ingham while trying to ask for her reaction to the first ballot of the 1990
party leadership contest. More recently he gained widespread public acclaim for
his appearance on *Strictly Come Dancing* which he eventually quit, fearing that his
comedic performance would jeopardise the chances of the more talented
contestants.

**As you had several different interests at university, comedy, theatre
and journalism, how did you know what it was you would dedicate
most of your time to?**

I suppose I had a choice between being a comic actor of some kind and
being a journalist and I always thought that journalism would be more exciting, I
thought we would travel the world, which in those days was quite difficult to do.
If you wanted to go to Vietnam for example, it was quite difficult to do that if
you were an ordinary person, whereas if you were a reporter, it was often
horribly easy to find yourself in Vietnam because that was the big war that was
going on at the time and there were a lot of reporters involved.

Were you ever scared?

There were lots of times I was scared and also I was persistently not brave. I think the mistake is to imagine that just because you have been to a war zone that makes you brave. No, it probably makes you frightened, it makes you nervous afterwards.

Were there any moments when you felt you were witnessing a particularly important moment in history?

I think there were lots of times when you knew it was an exceptional moment. I suppose the one that surprised me looking back was being there when Martin Luther King was making his 'I have a dream' speech in Washington and that was before I was a student or a journalist, and that sort of crept up on me. I did not know who Martin Luther King was and of course it wasn't a famous speech until very much later. It really became important, curiously enough, after he died, which was five years later.

How important was that period in Washington for you as a student, in terms of getting your thoughts together?

I think it was very important because I then realised, if I hadn't before, that I was pretty obsessed by politics and I was also very determined, I still am really, to try and work out what's going on and why so I suppose that stayed with me. There was an intense curiosity and that is what took me to Martin Luther King's speech, it was no coincidence that I was there. I had spent the whole summer thinking about race relations and the tensions in the American South and I was only 18 turning 19 so I suppose it was the realisation that this was a political obsessive in the making.

When you joined the BBC most of your colleagues in radio had not gone to university and would have had to work up through journalism. Do you think you can be a broadcast journalist now without having a degree?

No I think it is very difficult to be a broadcaster now without some kind of degree but then there are lots of different sorts of degrees aren't there? I always thought the main thing is for people to be quick-witted and work hard and it's very difficult to do that if you've not been at university, if you have managed to avoid university, it's quite a clever trick but I'm not sure what you would have been doing between the ages of 18 and 21 if you had that kind of application, and concentration too, to be successful in broadcasting.

When was the last time you spoke to Margaret Thatcher?

The last time I spoke to her, sadly, was in the 2001 General Election and she didn't know who I was, so that was sad. It was hardly a proper conversation, she did speak to me, I did speak to her but I don't think she was really able to work out where I was or how it all fitted in.

If you could ask her a question now, what would it be?

I suppose you would just want to go back over her feelings really, that is when she was at her best I think, when she was talking about what it was like at various points, I remember, right at the beginning of her time as Prime Minister, someone asked her if she would ever get over the excitement she said: "You can't be on cloud nine all the time, you've got to have some kind of discipline and habits." The way she responded was exactly as if she was some sort of housewife, she was very good at that, and she lost that towards the end of her time in Downing Street because she then tended to go on auto-pilot.

Do you think she became too confident in herself?

I think they get cut off and they get tired and they tend to find that the easiest evening for them is to perhaps talk to a group of people and just have a set speech which they then repeat to groups. She would say: "well what I'm thinking about at the moment..." and she'll suddenly launch into a lecture about North Sea oil and how it's refined and I'll think: "Why I am I being told this?" It's because she didn't want to talk about anything else and she did not want the conversation lead by somebody else, she would want to make sure she was leading a conversation and that was the easiest way to do it but it's irritating if you want a conversation with someone.

So you would want to get so some genuine feeling.

Yes you would want to get back some of that freshness and you would try to ask her anything such as "what was the first day like?" or "what do you feel about that?" and she would reply.

Was anyone particularly difficult to interview?

Lots of people are difficult to interview, John Prescott could be difficult. He was often annoyed with you or certainly annoyed with me. Denis Thatcher was impossible to interview, he thought I was a communist so that made it more difficult. I worked for the Bolshevik Broadcasting Company so that was trouble. Margaret Thatcher's first interview as PM was at 3am in the morning and I was at the back of a crowd of two hundred people and I realised the only way to get it, this was a radio interview, was to literally crawl under the feet of all these people, but I did it and I rose up in front of all them and she went "oh, surprising" and we went straight to the interview. So that's a difficult interview but on the other hand, one of the interviews I am particularly proud of.

Do you feel you have now gone comedy – journalism – comedy?

Yes, but in ordinary life people are often funny and then serious and people make jokes then they relax and people can accept that in an ordinary conversation so I don't know why people can't accept it when it comes to someone like me makes their living by talking.

It's difficult though when you are covering politics though because initially your producers and editors weren't particularly keen on you doing things like *Have I Got News For You?* were they?

That's right so you've got to be very careful about what you are actually doing at any given moment so if you are doing serious politics you can't be larking around because the audience won't trust you, which means you'll be bad at reporting politics. I was pretty determined to be good at it and that did not mean fooling about in the middle of Downing Street where as if you are on a comedy programme and you are not fooling about in Downing Street then you're no good, so you've got to be very careful to make sure are doing the right thing for the right programme.

Do you still think leaving *Strictly* was the right thing to do?

Oh yes, absolutely it was the right thing to do. The atmosphere was turning and you don't want to do something which is really going against the grain of the audience, why should you? It wasn't as if I had set my heart on winning *Strictly Coming Dancing*, it wasn't one of my great ambitions but having some fun and enjoying it was an ambition and I think I succeeded.

Have you done much dancing since *Strictly Come Dancing*?

No, no, it's not the sort of thing you can just go and do and also it's not like traditional dancing, you are learning a routine, so it's not really the same as going along to some dance hall and saying "will you dance with me?" I probably wouldn't know what to do.

Ashley Coates

Julian Dunkerton

Co-founder and CEO, Superdry

"Never think of yourself. It's about your staff, your customer, and your business. You're tenth on the list. If you're thinking that you are doing it for a Porsche then forget it, because you'll never make the right decisions to build the business".

The extraordinary growth of Superdry can in large part be credited to Julian Dunkerton's strict adherence to a number of core business principles that have started to reshape the way clothing and other parts of the retail sector work. Superdry's distinctive twist on British and American classic designs was inspired by a research trip to Japan, where Julian and his business partner became interested in the bright colours and bold text from Japanese packaging. Since it started trading, the company has received a number of key celebrity endorsements from David Beckham, Jamie Oliver and Leonardo DiCaprio amongst others. In March 2010 it floated on the stock market with a valuation of £400 million, by December it had a market capitalisation of £1.2 billion.

The co-founder of one of the most successful British business ventures in recent times is now thought to be worth an estimated £300 million. But Julian is no stranger to hard work. He started his business career at the age of 19, living off a £40/week government business grant and moving clothes from London to his shop in Herefordshire on the train. He sold his first shop to his business partner within a year and then moved to Cheltenham, where SuperGroup PLC still has its headquarters.

Julian remains thoroughly committed to the business, citing the drive to expand abroad as a major source of motivation for him. Above all else, Julian advises aspiring entrepreneurs to work hard and put the interests of the business above personal interests, keeping focused on staff, the needs of the consumer and the bottom line rather than the rewards that come with running a successful business.

How did you get into retail, having left school when you did?

I moved from London when I was 14, to Herefordshire, and I don't know if you know rural Herefordshire but there's not a lot going on. I took the wrong subjects at A-Level, Physics, Chemistry and Biology and I absolutely hated them. I stuck it out and got 3 Es so passed but very unattractively and just knew that it wasn't for me, and obviously that made university impossible, though I could have gone to a poly, but to do what? I took a year out, worked in factories and farms and so on to get the money to go traveling.

I had spotted this guy in my village who was selling carpets and he really impressed me, he was selling off-cut carpets and making a fortune in this little barn shop of his. I had done a few things before like burger wagons, and I enjoyed selling, my parents had a cider factory and I used to like selling in the farm shop and I worked out that I was good at it. So then it was a case of "what do I know that other people don't know?" Coming from London and spending my childhood buying clothes in Kensington Market and Camden Market I knew there was stuff that simply wasn't available in rural Herefordshire. At the time there was a scheme called the Enterprise Allowance Scheme, which was a government funded deal where you had to go unemployed for 13 weeks, which I did to get the £40/week that supported me while I started the business. I borrowed £2000 and I persuaded a guy to join me in opening a shop in Herefordshire. I literally went down to London, bought clothes from various wholesalers, brought them back and it took off.

That year, I paid back my loan to my family. I hate debt, I feel a massive moral obligation to pay it back, so I paid back the loan very quickly. Then the guy that I set it up with decided to join me running it and that didn't really work out, he quickly proved that he had no business skills whatsoever, so I decided to sell it to him. That was a year long process and I made £16,000, bearing in mind this was the mid-80s. I decided Cheltenham was the place where I wanted to settle, there wasn't too much competition and I repeated the same deal with my friend who had gone travelling with me, by which time it was called Cult Clothing Co. and I have been here ever since.

And it was through Cult that you began to develop the strategy that has served Superdry so well, the lack of in-store sales, the lack of advertising, and your own anonymity, it seems like a set formula, is it something you had to sit down and work out or was that your natural approach?

It's all very logical. Keeping a low profile so that nobody copied us, or copied me, as it was in the early days. Secondly, in terms of not having sales, having watched other business models, and building up other people's brands through the Cult brand I worked out that actually the traditional retail model was flawed. If you take the winter period it lasts from September till about March and if it gets very hot in March it's a rarity, so to put all your winter product on sale half way through the season is totally irrational and therefore it is built around

100

somebody else's conception of what makes logical business. People fall into this trap of not actually thinking for themselves, they emulate without thinking. You want people to buy Christmas products in your store and yet you devalue products the day after Christmas? That makes no sense to me. So I have tried to make stuff affordable all the way through the year so that you pick something up and go "it's worth it" rather than overpricing it for eight months and being on sale for months, that seems totally irrational.

You have talked about Superdry as a "global lifestyle brand", rather than a straight-forward clothing company. How far do you think you can take that idea? Could Superdry become an umbrella brand for a variety of different products...?

There's two ways you can bring about a "lifestyle brand", if you like, you have a core product that started the whole thing and then you license it out to lots of people and that's a trap that everyone falls into. So if you go into Company A, you'll pick up some shoddy item, you will find a shoddy version of a mediocre brand, such as a pair of glasses. Actually you've got to follow your philosophy through every product that you touch. We made a few mistakes at the beginning but now we're really getting total control of every product that we touch, and making sure that when you pick it up it's better quality than everyone else for the price that we're asking. So you should end up being a very happy consumer with every product that we get involved in. That's what it's all about.

Would you say that you have achieved a good work-life balance?

Surprisingly, over the past 30-odd years I think I've had an amazing work-life balance. I'm proud, I think, of being a good dad. I could probably do with some more fishing time but that's because I choose to spend all my spare time with my kids and my family. So I'll be home at 6 o'clock tonight and I will spend every weekend with my children.

I know you don't like talking about your own personal wealth but I think it would be interesting for people to know what motivates you to come into work. Because you have that choice, I think it would be fair to say, you could be doing other things.

The thing is with people like me, we love work. For this brand to conquer another country, to keep developing, to employ more people. I get excited by seeing products being created by the design team because I know it means progress. Progress is what I thrive on, so if you look at my history, I could have retired years ago but I would have gone mad! I like being challenged and there's nothing like the fashion industry for an intellectual challenge. It's never static. It's an adrenaline rush that you would find hard to achieve anywhere else. I'm not an object man, I don't need to own yachts. The thought of bobbing around on the Mediterranean for a week would drive me insane.

You have been noted for being quite conservative - with a small 'c' - with your spending.

Correct. I have had a philosophy for 28 years where I never spent anymore than 10% of what I earned, and like I say, objects don't concern me. My old philosophy was that so long as I could afford a round of drinks and a meal out then, what else do I need?

Is there any advice you would give to people, in their early twenties, looking to start a business?

You have to forget about objects and just try to be the best that you can possibly be in the niche that you think you have found. There are thousands of niches, it's just a case of finding yours. Never think of yourself. It's about your staff, your customer, and your business. You're tenth on the list. If you are thinking that you are doing it for material things, then forget it, because you'll never make the right decisions in business to build the business.

Is your specific route that you have taken something that you would advise others to follow? A lot of aspirational young people are beginning to consider university to be the default option.

I think it's very typical for people like me to have not been to university. If you look at the serious entrepreneurs in this country you will find that a huge number of them have not been to university and out of the entrepreneurs that have been to university they become entrepreneurs because often of their particular skills base, so they go down a very narrow channel.

You've talked about the importance of maintaining an interest in the news. Do you still find the time to read the newspapers?

As best I can. I do on any journey I am doing. On a normal working day I do not have time, I don't travel as much as I used to, I am more office bound than I used to be. I try to get a different political perspective as well. My natural paper is probably The Guardian in terms of politics but I read The Telegraph as well for different aspects of politics and for their business pages. I never indulged in supporting football teams because it would have taken too much of my time. I watch people and they go straight to the back pages and I'm thinking: "You've got to read the first 20 pages before you're allowed to read that!".

It's your treat! So have you been strict about which hobbies you have pursued?

Yes, very strict.

What's the next big thing that's going to hit the clothing industry in your opinion?

The most important thing is that it's doing what the car industry did over the last five decades. They were talking about historical car brands on Radio 4 this morning and what you've got now is total consolidation, so the independent multi-brand store, which is how I started, is going to disappear, virtually. It's going to become a difficult business. If you're a particular social group and buying into the car industry you might buy a Mercedes, or a BMW, or an Audi, or one of those brands that compete in that market. In another market you might be after a Bentley or a Rolls-Royce. Actually every segment is divided into a few brands, on a global scale but there's enough choice out there to keep everybody happy and that's what you are now seeing in the clothing industry. You are getting the consolidation of brands, if you like, owning particular parts of consumer behaviour.

Is there anything else you have on your radar? Any plans for a massive diversion into another area?

I own a few pub-restaurants. But no in terms of my main business - this is my main business. Probably this sector will always be my main business, I imagine. I started a coffee chain [Soho Coffee Co.] with James, my design partner at Superdry in a bored state. There are now more than 25 branches. My biggest love now is trying to work out what's best for the country. I used to stand for the local Labour council back in 1985. I feel very British, so I don't hide my money away in tax havens.

Well for one thing it was the enterprise allowance scheme that got your going so it would hardly be ethical!

It doesn't stop most people in my position! I'm probably a complete oddity to be honest but I feel very British, I feel very proud to be British and I want to pay all my taxes here but I also like calculating what the government should be doing to help the country.

Julian Fellowes DL
(Lord Fellowes of West Stafford)

Actor, screenwriter, novelist and film director.
Gosford Park, The Young Victoria, Downton Abbey, Snobs.

When Julian Fellowes started work on Gosford Park he had hardly expected it to be made into a film, let alone win the Best Original Screenplay category at the 2002 Oscars. On the face of it, that was an extremely improbable outcome, Gosford was Julian's first screenplay that had been made into a film and it was competing against both *Amélie* and *Memento*. As he said in his acceptance speech: "I feel as if I am in A Star is Born and any moment now Norman Maine is going to come out and whack me in the mouth."

The Oscar win was the reward for a lifetime of hard work and the pursuit of success in the entertainment industry that had started when Julian was a student. The theatre scene at Cambridge allowed him to explore both his interest in acting and his interest in the British class system. Away from the idyllic life he had enjoyed as a child, university introduced Julian to the full spectrum of human society, stimulating a fascination with class that has inspired many of his scripts. He had a successful acting career, appearing in *The Monarch of the Glen, Tomorrow Never Dies* and *The Aristocrats* and he maintained an active interest in writing throughout, producing scripts for children's TV in the UK. But it was Robert Altman and *Gosford* that gave Julian his big break in both writing and the film industry and over the next few years he penned a number of successful scripts including The Young Victoria.

In 2010, the first series of *Downton Abbey* aired on ITV and soon became one of the most popular series on television. In 2012, Downton won the "Best Mini-Series made for Television" category at the Golden Globes. Julian Fellowes became the Lord Fellowes of West Stafford in 2010 and he sits on the Conservative benches.

When you sit down to write a new piece of work, and you have a blank screen or piece of paper staring at you, how do you approach the task of creating new characters and plots, can you just sit there and write or do you need to wonder around to get inspiration?

I am a big believer that you must not wait until you are in the mood. You must have a discipline, you sit down and you write. Sometimes what you write is not very good and later you will correct it or rewrite it but you must write and start to fill that blank screen. I'm a believer in the principle of a day at a time. It's no good thinking "oh my God, what am I going to do with this whole series?". You've got to sit down and think, "today I am going do the beginning of Mrs Patmore's plot" or something like that. I also try to finish writing for the day when I know what comes next.

I don't think there is much value in going back and back and back because if you do that you will never get beyond page 30. You have to keep moving forward until you write "the end". That business of constantly correcting what you have already written, I think slows people down to a standstill if they are not too careful.

It must help to finish at least some part of it so as to get a perspective on what to do next?

Yes, and when you get to the end of a particular episode you can look back and see what is wrong with it much more clearly. You are not "in it" in the same way. When I have finished a first draft I get my wife to read it, I read her notes, then I'll get my agent to look at it, and I'll read her notes and then it goes on to a producer. When they come the production notes can be absolutely infuriating but if you just give it some time and you reread them you can see what they are getting at. Sometimes I disagree with them and sometimes they're wrong but there is far more in the notes that is good if you just give yourself some time to distance yourself from the material so you get more of a sensation of reading it for the first time. That's what I find anyway.

Does the pressure of working to a deadline help as well?

The pressure of episodic television is the greatest. With something like *Downton*, because I am the only writer, you start filming the series with something like four scripts in pretty good shape and maybe a fifth that needs another draft. But that leaves you with five or six hours of television still to write. Once the filming has begun then it becomes inexorable, because by the 18th they have to have the draft, by the 20th they have got to have the location and the wardrobe needs to know who is going to be in the next episode. As the series goes on, you are writing against time until finally, by the time you get to the Christmas Special, you are absolutely writing into the night and chewing your fingernails. That's real pressure, whereas with a film, although there is a lot of pressure, you don't start the film until everyone is content with the script. Then the whole shoot will last about 10 weeks and that's it, it goes into the edit, and you as a writer can essentially piss off.

Downton has many different facets to it that make it appealing, the intrigue within the household, the house itself and the historical themes in the background, are you consciously following a formula with Downton, or is it more a case of following your instincts?

I don't think I had a formula in mind except that the whole Altman experience had taught me that I, like him, enjoy the multi-strand narrative. I don't always have to write like that and there are films I have done that are not multi-strand. But I thought that was a very appropriate setup for *Downton*, having all these stories jiggling along,each of them driven by just a line here and a line there. I felt it was a way of reinventing the period drama by taking a structure that had been developed in American television shows, such as ER, and using it for a British period drama. Beyond that I think it was instinctive. It's a generous show, most of the people in it are nice people and even the ones that aren't nice like Thomas is not all bad. In that sense, it is about niceness in a way that had gone very much out of fashion in British television in particular. That was just me, I think most people, regardless of their background or economic circumstances are trying to do their best given the tools they have. So that is my philosophy translated into the show really.

Looking back to Oscar night in 2002, you seemed genuinely amazed to have won for Gosford.

I didn't really think that I had a chance. It seemed like the last act of a Julie Garland musical to write the first film that you have ever written that actually gets made and then to get the Oscar for it was just such an unlikely thing. *Gosford* was very, very successful but it was an art house picture in American terms, it wasn't a big franchise film, it wasn't *Titanic*. I just couldn't believe that it had been seen by enough people and made sufficient inroads to get that level of award but I was frightfully pleased that it did. It was the only Oscar for the film but I think in fact Robert Altman should have won. *A Beautiful Mind* is a very, very good film but I don't think it was as good as *Gosford* and I think over the years *Gosford* has stood up more than *A Beautiful Mind* in terms of lingering memory.

You also used your speech to apologise for being "mean and moody", is this really the case?

I am much more difficult in private life than I give the impression of on television. Like anyone who has featured on television quite a lot as themselves, you do develop a persona that works with that medium. It needs to be pretty much like the person you really are otherwise you couldn't keep it up but by the same token it isn't the whole person you really are. On television I think I come across as someone who is pretty good natured and well-tempered and so on whereas I am much more ill- tempered in real life. All the men in my family have filthy tempers, we're not sulkers, we just blow up. Also in the mix is the tension of having an enormous amount of stuff you are meant to be doing and everyone thinking that what you are doing for them is your primary commitment. Of course everyone is more complicated than their screen persona, but I hope I am reasonably truthful about my beliefs. I think the philosophies that I express, whether it is on *Question Time* or being interviewed here, are authentic. My reasonably benevolent liberal conservatism is probably the correct representation of what I believe.

Could you outline how you came to write the script for *Gosford*?

My script writing career had begun earlier when I drifted into it at the BBC in children's drama, which in those days was a separate department to the main drama department. I had targeted it originally to produce as I thought it would be easier to get into children's as a producer, which I think I was right about actually. I had written and co-produced a couple of shows and series there and then a different head came in and Anna Home, who had been my patroness, left. I started writing scripts for the first time in my life and I was doing them while I was still acting. One of them had been a version of Trollope's The Eustace Diamonds, which I wrote for a producer in America called Bob Balaban and in another part of his portfolio, Balaban was trying to set up a film with Robert Altman. Altman liked to take a fairly defined genre and make it Altman-esque, so he'd take a thriller, or a western and turn it into an Altman film. He wanted to do this with the country house murder mystery and originally they were looking at Tom Stoppard and Christopher Hampton and if any of those people had said yes you would probably be talking to Tom Stoppard now. But luckily for me none of them could do it. You also have to remember that at that time the received wisdom was that any kind of period show was dead, the public had lost interest and any examination of class belonged to the 1950s. So there was nothing very enticing about me for them except that I was working with Bob on what was probably going to be his only English film. Anyway, in the middle of trying to get the film moving and with all these refusals, Robert Altman was about to give up when Balaban suddenly remembered that I had written the Eustace script for him, and he just took a punt really. He said to Altman: "there's this guy, you won't have heard of him, he's never written a film that's got made but this is his sort of territory". I had one of those terrible transatlantic conference calls where you can't really hear anything anyone is saying and I was commissioned.

Originally this was only to write some character sketches, I think that was just so that Altman could see I was on the right track. As you can imagine, I put down the telephone and I rushed off to the video store and got out absolutely every Altman movie I could find and gave myself a sort of private Altman festival. From this, I learned that he specialised in a very specific multi-strand kind of movie. It would not be a single narrative at all. So I started to write on that basis and did some character sketches, quite a few of which ended up in the movie and then fairly seamlessly I was asked to write a first draft. I have to say at no point did I think it would get made at that stage because Altman hadn't had a success for quite a long time and this wasn't his stamping ground. If someone had wanted to put some money into a classic Altman movie, this wouldn't have been it. By the same token, I realised if it did get made, it would be my lucky break to end all so I had to give it everything I'd got in case it was made. It sounds rather odd to say it like that but that was my thinking. It wasn't really until I had sent it and then Bob Altman read it and I was flown out to California to work with him for two or three days that I began to think: "oh I wonder if it really might happen," because it seemed like they were putting their money where their mouth was.

After that it all moved incredibly fast. I think I was asked to do it in January 2000, in September Bob came to London and in November he moved to London and we started shooting the following March. In film terms, that was quick. I got so caught up in it that the extraordinary nature of what was taking place in my life receded. When you are on set all you can think of is "this luggage is wrong, we need to find new suitcases". You don't really look at the broader picture. For me it came much later because at the time I was appearing in a BBC show called *The Monarch of the Glen* and I was supposed to be taking part in a new series. By this time Altman had asked me to be with him on the set of *Gosford* every day, which is very unusual for a writer but he wanted to protect himself and prevent any silly mistakes from happening. I said to the *Monarch* people that I could not miss out on this experience so I could not do this year in *Monarch* and they said they would put all my scenes together and move them back, to make it possible. Bob Altman used to say: "we've got lightning in a bottle" and in a way I thought we did have lightning in a bottle. From then on, it all happened pretty quickly because the day after New York opening, we flew out to los Angeles to open it there, and all before December 31st, which is the cut-off for Awards nominations.

I went off to see *Memento* which was the nomination for Christopher Nolan and of course it's an absolutely brilliant film and a brilliant script and to be quite honest if it had won the Oscar I don't think it would have been at all unjust. So I just assumed that *Memento* would be the winner and I got my face all set because the film crews like to run up to you and get a picture of you looking disappointed so you fix a Cheshire Cat grin on your face so you don't look furious. But I did win and it was a big surprise.

You've talked before about the incredible impact of winning the Oscar in 2002. In what ways was winning the Oscar at that particular stage in your career particularly impactful?

Period drama was always going to be my calling card and the received wisdom was that it was finished as a genre and so it was also extraordinary that somehow this part of the market that everyone thought was over came back in spades in order for me to continue living this sort of dream. That has been quite amazing. When a big star wins an Oscar, like when Julia Roberts won for *Erin Brockovich*, it was completely deserved but she was already a big star so I don't think her career altered. Whereas with me, the door of the wardrobe opened and out of the darkest recesses stepped this fat little balding Englishman that nobody had ever heard of, who walks up to the podium and takes the Oscar.

In that sense, there was a fairytale element to it. I became the "President of the Last Chance Saloon", but I was proud to be and I did have a very strong sense that it was the awareness that it was probably my last chance to have a big career that made me robust on the set. Sometimes people say to me "would you rather have made it when you were 30 rather than 50?" and of course the short answer is yes but the long answer is I am not sure I would have done because on the set I used to argue with Altman, I didn't always win but I did stick up for the script and I did stick up for the fact that I knew a lot more about this period and these people than he did, by his own admission. I don't think at 30 I would have had the nerve to do that, I would have just stood there, biting my tongue and feeling depressed. I did have a very strong feeling, that if I couldn't make this work and make this film as good as it could be then it wasn't going to change my life. I had that hovering over my head throughout the whole thing. In that sense being 50 was helpful to me.

Do you have any life philosophies you have followed and how do you account for your own success?

That's a hard question to answer really because I don't think anybody can account for their own success. Obviously in some way you have filled a need, just like the person who invents some new gadget that suddenly everyone has to own. Suddenly he or she has identified a gap in the market and I think I filled a gap in the market for a certain kind of decent television. That sounds rather pretentious but I don't think many other people were doing what I was doing at that time. When Peter Fincham first got behind *Downton* everybody thought he was mad. He was told there was no audience for this stuff by some very senior figures in the industry. He didn't agree with them, thank God, and he was right. I don't want to be too modest. What I am doing in this area I must be doing reasonably well because other people are now producing similar stuff in pursuit of our audiences but they are not all producing shows that are as successful as *Downton*. There must be some quality in the way I am writing these stories that works. The only thing I would say, and it sounds immodest but I hope it's helpful, is that I was a very, very hard worker, right from the start. To get an acting career going I wouldn't let a 24-hour period go by without doing *something*, whether that be writing a letter, or arranging an interview, or making a telephone call, and I kept that up for 10 years.

When I write, I write a lot. Some people have great difficulty putting pen to paper, some far more talented people than I am, have trouble getting on with it, but I have always been a very hard worker. In fact, I am now more or less a workaholic and my wife's great difficulty is to stop me working. If we go on holiday and I stop working I am like a drunk in need of a bar. And in truth I think that for most people, when they are successful, a lot of work is a big part of it.

There may be models spotted just standing waiting for a bus but in my experience even with something like modeling the ones that last are the ones that take the trouble to understand their own industry and how to develop what they've got and create new opportunities. I think that is true of artists and bankers, of Prime Ministers and Page 3 girls. One of the things that slightly irritates me about reality television is it promotes this notion that you can just be in the right place at the right time and you can become a star. It's not that I begrudge them, I just think it sends the wrong message out to young people, when what they have really got to do is work like stink.

Malcolm Walker CBE

Co-founder and CEO, Iceland.

"I had gone to sleep but I woke up and fired 60 per cent of our senior management,
60 per cent of our board of directors and got going again."

In February 1971, Iceland became Malcolm's full-time occupation after his employer, Woolworths, discovered he and his business partner were operating a frozen food business "on the side". Malcolm and another trainee from Woolworths had started a small business of their own in the previous year. In January 2009, Woolworths Group went into liquidation and two months later Malcolm's frozen foods venture reported record sales of just over £2 billion. It's an extraordinary journey for the former Woolies employee who started out sweeping the floor and weighing potatoes in the stock room. Today he is thought to be worth in the region of £215 million.

Malcolm attributes part of his success to a compulsion to achieve and to make money that was evident from a very early age. As a teenager he organised local discos for his neighbourhood in rural Yorkshire. Iceland, a business which today boasts over 800 stores and 25,000 employees, was started with only £30 his own money. The profits from his first week of trade were jotted on the back of an envelope, £370, no mean feat for a startup business in 1971. The costs to cover property and equipment rental were all covered by the sales just a few months after the first shop opened in Oswestry, Shropshire. Iceland achieved growth every year for 30 years and increased its profits in all but one of the years under his leadership. In 2001, the business entered a difficult patch when Malcolm was removed following a merger with the Booker Group. The merger had made Iceland-Booker one of the biggest food buyers in Europe but under new management, the casual ethos that had served the business so well was abandoned and replaced with a level of corporate orthodoxy that did not suit the company. Iceland suffered from a series of profit warnings and its share price plummeted. The company languished for four years before Malcolm returned in 2005. Within a year Iceland was achieving profits once more.

Iceland's size could lead you to assume that it's run in the manner of a similarly sized company but it's managed more in the style of a family business than a corporate giant. It is, in Malcolm's words a "simple business" that heavily invests in its workforce. Iceland is routinely in the lists of the best companies to work for, often winning them. Malcolm is proud of his company's record of employee satisfaction as well as its considerable charitable contributions. In 2011 he climbed the North Col of Everest and successfully abseiled 310 metres down the Shard in London in 2012.

Could you describe how your entrepreneurial instincts developed while you were working at Woolworths?

Well, can you learn to be an entrepreneur? Or is it there? We had nothing going on in the village where I grew up so to break the boredom I organised a dance in the church hall and then I ended up organising a series of dances, booking the church hall and hiring a band. I didn't do very well at school and failed to get into Marks & Spencer, Littlewoods and John Lewis, but Woolworths would take anybody. Their training programme was on the job, you started at the bottom in the stock room sweeping the floor and hoped to become directors. Everyone apart from lawyers and accountants had started out sweeping the floor.

It was hugely long hours, six or seven days a week and they moved you around the country. It was all about perseverance and the dropout rate was enormous. One of the things I had to do was weigh seed potatoes in the stock room. If there were too many I would take some of them home to our smallholding, plant them, and then sell them on to the canteen at Woolies. What I am trying to say to you is there is an inherent desire to do things and to make money I suppose.

And it wasn't a desire that could be fulfilled in the stock room at Woolies.

Seven years later, I was still in Woolies, and I hadn't done very well, I hated my job and I still hadn't become a manager. One day I was out with a friend of mine who also worked there and we saw a strawberry seller on the side of the road packing up and on some impulse we bought his strawberries. The next morning we went to a local beauty spot, sold the strawberries, and went to the pub to spend the money. That made us consider whether we should be trying other things. We tried out a few more ideas which didn't really work but then we decided to open a shop. We had absolutely no money so we couldn't open a shop that required a lot of stock, like a shoe shop, it would have cost a fortune. I had seen loose frozen foods for sale in a department store but in 1970 nobody had a freezer, not in the north of England anyway. Supermarkets only had small fridges with Birdseye in them. This shop I found had catering packs of peas, burgers and fish fingers, all tipped into plastic washing up bowls at the bottom of a freezer and sold them by the shovel full. So we decided to copy that.

We started this shop, putting down £60 in advance of a months rent and that was the only money we ever put into the business. We got two fridges, a cash register and a scale on hire-purchase, without having to pay a deposit. We found a local frozen food supplier who gave us credit for a week, which was then stretched to a month, so we were able to open the shop for £60. I couldn't get any time off work so I went sick for three days and my partner had three days holiday. We opened the shop and then at the end of the week we went to Woolies and carried on. Woolies found out about three months later and they fired us.

How were you able to start the business with so little money?

We found to our surprise that we had discovered something called positive cash-flow. We only needed £60 to set it up and we had a month's sales in the bank before we had to pay anybody. Every time we opened a shop our bank balance went up until we started spending more money on fitting out the shops and getting a bit posher. It's been incredibly easy because in the first 12 months we opened four shops and over the next three-or-four years we opened 20-odd loose frozen food shops which gradually got bigger and bigger as we started introducing packeted products. Without realising it we turned into a different business. We stopped doing the loose food. By this time people were buying freezers to put in the garage and they were buying frozen food in bulk.

Iceland showed an impressive rate of growth in the 1970s and 1980s but the retail market proved to be more hostile in the 1990s, what did you do to try to differentiate the business from some of its rivals on the high street?

We increased our profits every day from the day I started in 1970 to 1996 and we had our first ever profit set back then. It wasn't significant, we went from £173 to £165 million net profit but by this time we were a public company and of course the world collapsed, our share price collapsed and our market capitalisation went from £800 million to £140 million, yet we were making £120 million if you added our profit and depreciation together. So it was a complete overreaction as far as the market was concerned but they just saw that blip in profits as the beginning of the end. The City couldn't understand why we existed and felt we had past our sell-by date.

The reason why we had that first profit dip is, frankly, we went to sleep. We got a bit complacent and we got fat and lazy. I had gone to sleep but I woke up and fired 60 per cent of our senior management, 60 per cent of our board of directors and got going again. We introduced a number of innovations like home delivery and we got the company growing again. But by 1998-99, we had become a bit too big and a bit too democratic. I was probably getting tired and we were losing focus. There were too many committees and too much bureaucracy and we did loose our way. I was just looking forward to retiring, which was the prime motivation for our takeover of Booker. It was supposed to give me a new managing director called Stuart Rose. After the merger we went from having sales of £2 billion to £5 billion because Booker had £3 billion. You might wonder where the synergy was in combining Iceland with Booker and on the face of it there was none except buying power behind the scenes. Iceland-Booker became the largest buyer of Coca-Cola in Europe.

There were great synergies but Stuart Rose had only done the deal so that he could make an exit. He jumped ship just three months before I retired which I was a bit pissed off about. So I recruited this new guy called Bill Grimsey who did a lot to change the business but not in the right way. He put out a profit warning which was completely fictitious. For the next four years it should have been dead easy.

But it turned out to be a disaster. What went wrong?

Our management style is a bit chaotic, I describe myself as a cowboy. We run the business on the hoof and Grimsy was into corporate procedure and nothing ever got done. In the four years he was here we lost 25% of our sales, profits became negative and when we came back into the business four years later it had a £300 million bank overdraft. I came back with some investment people and took the company private. We sold off Booker, sold off Woodwoods and sold off a few properties. I didn't really know if it would be possible to turn the company around. One of the primary reasons why I came back was to get my hands on the books and see what had been going on and try to vindicate myself. I had only been back in the business for about three days before I realised it was going to be a complete piece of piss to sort it out because every single part of the business had been comprehensively screwed up. Our five year plan was really a handful of phrases: focus, simplicity and accept reality.

It seems to be a triumph of intuition over corporate orthodoxy.

Absolutely, I'm not suggesting our management style would run a big complicated company but it works for our business. When we came back there was no way we were going to be democratic, this is an autocracy, it's the Saddam Hussein School of Management. We had to make lots of changes but now we have the best management team we've had in many years.

You've talked about the business being "run on the hoof", how does that work in practice? Is it a case of dealing with things as they come along?

Yes no one can predict the future, you can have a five year plan but it's out of date as soon as you've done it. But you've got to have some sort of idea as to where you are going. We change our annual budget every week, we do it for the year but then it's constantly evolving. I suppose intuition does come into it a lot and just keep everything simple.

Iceland has been recognised for its positive corporate ethos, winning the Sunday Times Best Big Company to Work For award in 2012. What does the company do to foster its in-house culture?

We've got 25,000 staff, most of them are women and most of them are part-time. We're the second best payer on the high street. Can you believe that we pay better than Asda, Morrisons, John Lewis and Marks & Spencer? Still, £6.75 an hour is bugger all. One of the questions on the Best Big Company to Work For survey, which is totally anonymous, is "how do you rate your salary?" and we came number one on that, number two was Goldman Sachs. So our staff, at £6.75 an hour are more happy with their pay packet than people at Goldman Sachs, now how can that be? It's because it isn't just about the amount that you pay, it's about buying into the job. When I came back in 2005 we were a minimum wage employer. Our managers were among one of the worst paid on the high street and people were leaving the company in droves. Half the light fittings weren't working. What's the first thing you do when you buy a second hand car? You clean it. So when we came back in we cleaned the shops, repainted them, got the chewing gum off the floor and put some pride back into the place. The staff could see things were changing. We simplified their workload and took away a lot of the paperwork that existed before, so they were more motivated and worked better and then we could start some of the pay increases.

Our managers are now the best paid in the high street for the store that they're running. Our store managers now earn £35-40,000 a year, our area managers will be on £65-70,000 with a car. It's much harder to motivate your frontline staff who are on £6.75 an hour. Really, the pay isn't even half of it, it's the informality of the business and the fun you have in the business. Lots of businesses have fun as one of their keywords, well it might be fun for the bosses but not very much for the staff. We have a conference every year which is a massive jamboree for store managers and senior managers and each year it gets more and more ambitious. Three years ago we took a thousand managers to Disney World in Florida and we chartered three jumbo jets to take them. If you were a public company you would never be able to do that. We didn't have to justify that to anybody. Do we spend that £4 million and spread it thin and give everyone a pay-rise or do we give them a trip of a lifetime which they have never experienced before and will talk about six months afterwards? Every year we are doing parties, and conferences, not just for managers but for store staff. Four times a year we have area meetings. We spend a lot of money on fun but every penny is an investment because happy staff means happy customers and happy customers means cash in the till, it's as simple as that. I'm not altruistic, I'm doing it for financial reasons. I talk to other bosses about this and they half-nod in agreement but you could never really convince them. I would say that is 50 per cent of the reason for our success.

Martha Lane Fox CBE

(Baroness Lane-Fox of Soho)

Entrepreneur, philanthropist, public servant
Co-founder, Lastminute.com.

"We need scaled, extraordinary, businesses in this country, we have lots of brilliant entrepreneurs but we do not manage to scale our businesses very often. We need people to be bold and believe they can".

Martha Lane Fox is an icon of the dot com boom. She co-founded Lastminute.com with Brent Hoberman in 1998, back when the widespread use of the internet was far from being a certainty. By 2000, it was one of the most popular consumer destinations on the web and was floated on the London Stock Exchange with a valuation of £571 million.

Martha's school ventures echo her lifelong interests in business, innovation and public service. She started an in-house dating agency at her school and tried to get the teachers to take her colleagues to prisons as part of their volunteer programme. Martha would later express an interest in being a prison governor but graduated from Oxford with a degree in Classics and History before joining Spectrum, a consulting firm for IT and media companies. It was there that she met Brent and started developing the idea for an online travel and leisure retailer. Martha left Lastminute.com in 2003 to focus on her philanthropic activities and chose to use the notoriety and wealth gained from the Lastminute.com venture to pursue numerous charitable interests, setting up a grant trust called Antigone and promoting several digital inclusion initiatives. In 2009 she became the government's Digital Inclusion Champion, overseeing a campaign to make more people in the UK computer literate and using the internet constructively.

By 2011 Lastminute.com was reporting 1.65 million unique users per week. Martha became a crossbench life peer in the House of Lords in March 2013, taking the name Baroness Martha Lane-Fox of Soho in the City of Westminster. In so doing, Martha became the youngest woman member of the Lords and revived a title that had previously been held by her great aunt, Felicity Lane-Fox. She is also on the boards of Channel 4 and Marks & Spencer.

Was there any evidence of your interest in technology and business when you were growing up?

Not really, I was always very lucky because my parents were unbelievably supportive of me and everything I was trying to do. My father is an academic but also self-published his own books, wrote a gardening column and had a variable working life. My mum worked in a small business so I had lots of examples of different things going on around me and they would probably have had a heart attack if I had become an accountant or something like that. As far as tech was concerned, no, I was a classical historian so technology was far away from my universe but I did always like new ideas and innovation. I tried to innovate at my school by starting a dating agency but it didn't go very well, nobody wanted to pay for my services.

But you were in an environment where you were being encouraged to do things differently.

Exactly, and then for my first job by complete serendipity I ended up in a strategy consulting company which was in the nexus of media, tech and telecoms and that was where I began to understand that you could be smart and be in business as there were lots of knotty problems to be solved.

You once aspired to be a prison governor. What was the thinking behind that?

I think the thinking behind that is quite evident in what I have gone on to do in my professional life. I have always done a mix of public stuff and private stuff. I had always been interested in public service, if you like, and I also had an interest in criminal justice, I used to write to prisons when I was at school. I also tried to change the community service while I was at school so that we could go and visit prisons which didn't go very well. I was very serious about trying to get into the Home Office and I actually got through the fast-track exam but then I thought at the final hurdle: "no actually, you would go completely nuts", but I have been able to keep up a life-long interest.

Remarkably, you've been able to combine a public and a private role.

Yes I have been extremely lucky.

Back in 1998, barely 8% of the UK was connected to modems. Could you outline what the online market was like back then?

Yes Brent and I were not only trying to convince people that Lastminute.com would survive and thrive but also that the internet wouldn't blow up. We had conversations with investors and suppliers where they would be asking us whether we really believed it would survive and be something that would be a proper channel. That was the real battle and we were partly fighting it for our own business and partly fighting it for the sector. The speeds were incredibly slow and there were many copies of American businesses arriving in the UK but there was no Facebook, no Google, no Twitter, Amazon was only just beginning, it was a very different landscape.

What were the steps needed to get Lastminute.com off the ground in this environment?

It is really important to understand that it was Brent's idea. He had the eureka moment and he very generously asked me to join him and made me co-founder. He did the initial research and it was born out of his needs as someone who was always going away on last minute breaks. It's really important to me that people know he is the driving force behind the initial idea. When you start something you are operating on every axis, you are trying to find people, make technology work, trying to raise money, you just have to go full-pelt at everything and it's really bloody difficult. There's no short answer to this. We wrote a business plan and then had to take it to a consulting company, we then tried to raise the money which took a long time, we built the platform which was pretty shocking because it was the first incarnation of it, called hotels, airlines and suppliers endlessly to try and get products, build the team and try to get out there at every available opportunity to tell people about the internet and Lastminute.com.

Having never sought fame before, you very suddenly became a poster girl for the UK dot-com boom. You also became very wealth, very quickly. How much did your life change as Lastminute.com took off?

You know, we were working so freaking hard at this time. I would occasionally go out and someone would say, "hello Martha!" and I would be a bit surprised that somebody knew my name. Our entire focus, 20 hours a day, was trying to make the company work, even when the nonsense about the dot-com crash was out there and people were writing pretty nasty things about me. It was a funny kind of thing and I think only in the last few years of my life have I been able to see the many benefits as well as the disadvantages of the tiny bit of notoriety I had.

Was it difficult to manage that notoriety when it first began?

It was difficult when Brent was cut out of the photos and it was all about me. Then I got sent loads of letters after the share price collapsed, the nicest of which was, "you're a bitch". It was hard.

Before the sudden media interest were you particularly conscious of your appearance being quite different to most of the people in tech?

Because I'm a woman you mean?

Yes.

I think that helps, I would be completely nuts if I didn't recognise that it has been helpful but at the same time, you had to build your credibility. It's a double-edge sword but generally of course it helps.

It's not unusual for successful entrepreneurs to get involved in philanthropy but for you good causes have become your main activities. Which issues have grabbed your attention the most?

In 2009 I took on a role with the government focusing on helping people get digital skills. I never imagined that I would survive more than a few months working for the government. It has now been four years and we've had this astonishing roller coaster and now we've got charities and the corporate sector involved. I've loved it, I've been incredibly lucky in having made money from Lastminute.com and I'm not driven to make more. I don't invest furiously in commercial enterprises, I'm interested in public service. I think it goes back to things I was interested in early in my life. If I can do something for the good of other people in some small way then that is incredibly fulfilling for me personally.

Many people assume that Britain is a very connected place and everyone is using emails, word processing applications and the like with ease. But during your time as the government's digital commissioner, you have found that many of us are barely using the internet. What has been done to help bring these people into the fold?

Very simply, three things, one is dramatically changing the way the government provides services online, so that's the Gov.uk site. I built a network of companies that I would get to do stuff, so it was a more B2B [business to business] approach, rather than just trying to get people to take part. Then I built a network of champions, so as much as I am a "UK champion", I tried to make sure there are individual champions, whether that is in a Post Office, or within a family, or an office. It's that peer-to-peer network that I think will grow constructive use of the internet.

You named your grant foundation Antigone, after a character from Greek mythology. Could you tell me a bit about Antigone and why it was chosen as the name for your charitable foundation?

She is a fictional Greek classical hero who stood up for what she believed in and ultimately paid the worst possible price with her life when she was executed for demanding that her brother had a proper burial. As a classical historian and a feminist and, hopefully, a relatively strong woman despite the accident, she has always been an easy person to look to for good values.

How do you account for your own success?

Lots of help, I think this notion that it's the individual and the cult of the entrepreneur troubles me somewhat. I don't know many entrepreneurs that don't have an amazing team around them and I was incredibly lucky that I have always had a great team around me. Brent is a really remarkable person, my family is really remarkable, my boyfriend has been extraordinary. I really mean that very profoundly, it's made life a lot more fulfilling and I have been a lot more successful than if I had been alone. Obviously it is hard to praise yourself but I hope I have a not-totally-self-aware optimism so what I like to think is I believe in the possible. My default reaction is let's go for it, let's be bold, let's be ambitious, let's try to change the world rather than just try to edge forward. If you get wheeled back a bit then that's okay. I try to do it with self-awareness and by that I mean, not being unpleasant to people, not being ego-led, trying to be generous and a decent person to be around.

Would you say you have achieved a good work/life balance?

I really don't know what that is and I don't mean to sound facetious in saying that. I don't have kids and I think that is an important thing in the mix and I am aware that I am talking from a very different position to many women and men. I do struggle every day with the consequences of a very serious car crash so that forces you to work in a slightly different way. Having said that, I am always switched on, I probably do think about things too much and work too much but I am also lucky in that I can organise my own life and I don't have to go into an office at eight in the morning and leave at eight at night. I can choose how I run my life so I really don't know what that means if that's not too disingenuous.

What advice would you give to someone who is interested in starting

their own business?

The first thing is that the world of not-for-profit social good and the commercial sector are colliding at a rapidly accelerating pace and I would urge people at the beginning of their business to just think about the mixed model. What can you embed in your business that will contribute to society as well as the commercial model that you might have? Another aspect to this is, starting in 2013, whether your business is an online business or an offline business, you have to embed technology at the heart of it, how you think about your communications, how you talk to your suppliers, how you present yourself on the web, you just cannot be online or offline, you have to think about the digital core of what you do, even if you are selling meat in a butchers. Also, be bold, we need scaled, extraordinary, businesses in this country, we have lots of brilliant entrepreneurs but we do not manage to scale our businesses very often. We need people to be bold and believe they can. Finally, hire astonishing people, get the absolute best.

Sir Martin Sorrell

CEO, WPP Group

"I have an emotional commitment: if we win something I take it personally, if we lose something I take it personally, if somebody joins us I take it personally, if somebody leaves us I take it personally. It's beyond just a job".

For anyone unfamiliar with WPP it may come as a surprise that the world's largest advertising firm started off as Wire and Plastics Products plc, a British company selling wire shopping baskets. Looking for a corporate "shell" in which to grow the business, Martin, formerly finance director at Saatchi & Saatchi, bought a stake in the company in 1985. He surprised both the communications and business world with a string of major acquisitions, taking over some of the oldest and most prestigious advertising companies in the world. By 2013, WPP was employing over 170,000 people worldwide and had revenues of £10.4 billion. Martin himself is now thought to have a net worth of more than £200 million and is the second longest-standing FTSE 100 CEO.

He is a graduate of Christ's College, Cambridge and has an MBA from Harvard. He remembers his childhood fondly, learning business skills from his father, a retailer who ran a large chain of stores in the 1960s. He joined Saatchi & Saatchi in 1975 where he became known as "the third brother", a reference to his close working relationship with Maurice and Charles, the two co-founders who had fostered a reputation for groundbreaking creativity as well as making bold business acquisitions.

Today Martin is one of the world's most respected and recognisable businessmen, regularly commenting on financial and economic issues. Keenly aware that he is witnessing a time of considerable upheaval within the advertising world as well as the media as a whole, Martin makes sure to keep abreast of the latest technological developments that have been rapidly reshaping the industry. Far from being just a holding company, the structure of WPP allows it to support and grow the companies in its roster, providing financial, legal and strategic support as well as giving its constituent firms the opportunity to pool resources. At the time of writing the companies that form WPP are working with all 30 of the Dow Jones 30, 63 of the NASDAQ 100 and 350 of the Fortune Global 500.

You grew up in North London, where your father was a very

successful businessman himself. To what extent did that experience influence the direction you took later in life?

I used to read the *Financial Times* when I was about 13 going to school on the bus from Mill Hill to Haberdashers' so I had an early interest. My father was a retailer and I was very interested in what he was doing. He ran the equivalent of Dixons in the 60s with about 750 stores in the UK so I used to talk a lot about business with him and on Sundays we would get the sales manager's reports and visit the shops with him.

He also ran a retail division of an industrial holding company called Firth Cleveland which was run by a guy called Sir Charles Hayward. Charles was essentially a metal-basher from Wolverhampton and after the war he went into retail, starting one of the first publically quoted industrial conglomerates in this country. He had a wonderful estate in Sussex and I remember one afternoon when I was about 14 he asked me "what do you want to do when you grow up?" and I said I wanted to go into business. He told me "well you must go to Harvard Business School", which really stuck in my mind and I later did go to Harvard.

My father was also very close to Sir Jules Thorne, a Viennese Jew who founded Thorne Electrical Industries. He landed in the UK with nothing and built a fluorescent lighting factory in Enfield. He was a very good mentor and a lovely man, like a little peanut really, he always took an interest in me. So there was a bit of business background. I also did Economics A-Level and Economics at Cambridge. I went to Harvard Business School where I was part of what was called "the most naïve class at Harvard" because most of the students were trying to avoid the draft.

You maintained that very close relationship with your father right the way through, including the beginnings of WPP.

One of my bigger regrets is that we never did anything together. We did try for a couple of months but it was absolutely hopeless. If it had worked it would probably have been even more fun than what I ultimately have done. Despite being busy he always had time for everyone and I would speak to him three to five times a day even in the most extreme of circumstances. In the depths of the JWT and Ogilvy deals in 1987-89 I would speak to him all the time.

You mentioned your time abroad at Harvard but you also went travelling with the now world-renowned historian Simon Schama in 1963.

I went to the Atlantic City Convention when Lyndon Johnson was facing down Barry Goldwater, then the following year went to East Berlin, Prague and Vienna and on to Budapest. So we saw the West and the East. We were traveling when there was still the Iron Curtain and you had to go through Checkpoint Charlie. So we saw both sides of the coin but we had a wonderful time in America at the Convention as reporters for the university student newspaper.

Was that a particularly formative experience?

I think it was very formative in terms of trying to understand America and learning a bit more about the East because at the time of course East Berlin, Prague and Budapest were pretty depressing places to be honest. Obviously they have changed immensely since the fall of the wall. It was formative in the sense of understanding a bit about East and West and admiring the changes that have gone on in the East since the wall came down.

Leading up to the beginning of your role at WPP, you had a very successful career that included working at Saatchi & Saatchi, where you became finance director in 1977. Most of the entrepreneurs I have interviewed for this series have tended to launch their companies earlier in their lives and often don't have a professional background. What motivated you to start the WPP project at this particular time?

Are you trying to politely say I was an old man?

I, well.

Yes I suppose I would like to have started it five years earlier but Saatchi's was a good training ground and I could do pretty much what I wanted to there with freedom so long as there wasn't too much publicity about it. It was the largest agency in the world at that time, and I was, I would say immodestly, a key part of that and it was a great experience. But 40 is a pretty pivotal point, you look back over the first 20 years of your career and you look at the next 20. My father always said you should fashion a reputation for yourself in an industry you enjoy, it doesn't have to be a public reputation, and then go from there. So aged 40 I borrowed £250,000 from the bank against my Saatchi shares.

I know we have touched on this already but are there any particularly key bits of advice your father gave you that really stuck in your mind?

I think that one of them was that you shouldn't flit from one opportunity to another, you should stick to one industry that you enjoy. He would describe himself as a cart-horse, left school at 13 and was the youngest of five. Hard work, commitment, eye for detail, these are all attributes he had. He was passionately interested in what he did but also very family orientated.

Many people who are not familiar with the sector would be surprised to learn that "WPP" stands for Wire and Plastic Products, and that the firm originally produced wire shopping baskets. Could you outline how and why you went about gaining control of the company?

There was a guy called Preston Rabl who wanted to invest jointly with me which he did initially and we bought about 12.5% of the company each and then I upped it to 29.9%. We wanted a small manufacturing company where the management was "mature but not senile", was the phrase that we used. We were looking for a firm that had a simple manufacturing process that had not lost money and we could understand and could work with. It had to have a good freehold property so no stresses and strains, no debt, and we alighted on Wire and Plastic Products. It was a great piece of luck that the advisers to Wire and Plastic were Panmure Gordon as the broker, who I had worked with when I was working for James Gulliver and also County Bank, who were bankers to Saatchi's.

When we first approached WPP, we went to see Gordon Sampson, the Managing Director, at the wire works. We were absolutely starving so we went off and bought some fish and chips and Gordon was convinced we had done it because we wanted to be seen as "men of the people", which we hadn't, we were just hungry. So Gordon rang County Bank and said "do you know this bloke, Sorrell?" and they were in a difficult position because they acted for Saatchi's and felt they had a conflict of interest.

The guy said to Gordon, "let me think about it overnight and I'll come back to you tomorrow morning" so he called back in the morning and said "all I can say to you is I can't give you advice one way or another, just let me tell you a story". He told Gordon a story about Greg Hutchins who was an acolyte of Slater Walker who did a similar shell idea with a company called Tomkins. Greg bought the shares at 10p and after the first day's trading the shares were at 15p. So Gordon got the message that it was a deal he should do because it would add value to the business and we were off to the races. But the point of the story is, just like when we took over JWT in 1987 and found a building Morgan Stanley had valued at $30 million which we then sold for $207 million, some of this is about luck and good fortune.

JWT is 150 years old next year and was 125 years old when we bought it. So on another level you could actually say it's not luck, you could say that when you buy a company that is 125 years old the odds are there is something there that somebody has forgotten about, a tangible or intangible asset, the value of which is in excess of the book value. What they were doing at JWT was depreciating a freehold; they had a freehold property which in those days used to depreciate by 2.5% per year because those were the accounting rules. So that had been depreciated to nothing when it was actually worth $200 million. Our bid price was $525 million, so 40% of the value was lying in this property in Tokyo.

Was it difficult to get the investment needed to make some of your bigger acquisitions, thinking about JWT, Ogilvy and Mather and Young and Rubicam?

It was never difficult to do the deals, it was more difficult to make them work. It was never difficult to get the money. We made big mistakes, for example I made a big mistake in 1989 by over-leveraging the Ogilvy acquisition, because it was $825 million, there was no Tokyo property to take out the debt and I did it half debt, half convertible preferred* and I forgot that in a recession, convertible preferred becomes debt. So I made a bit of a boo-boo there and it wasn't easy. You have your luck and you make your mistakes. We acquired Ogilvy in 1989, went into recession in 1991-92 and had to restructure the company, but I felt I was the one that got us into that mess so I had to get us out again so I stuck at it.

You were once quoted as saying: "WPP is not a matter of life or death, it's more important than that."

That's a plagiarism of Bill Shankly's quote, it sits on my desk and it's something like "football is not a matter of life or death, it's much more important than that" so I just substitute WPP for football.

What significance does that quote in particular have for you?

Founders have an emotional attachment that managers or turnaround artists don't have. I have an emotional commitment: if we win something I take it personally, if we lose something I take it personally, if somebody joins us I take it personally, if somebody leaves us I take it personally. It's beyond just a job.

The media often says that you're always busy and very restless and

have to keep active. Is this really the case or is it a bit of a caricature?

You can ask others but I think that probably is the case. I am very focused on the business, probably too focused. Some would say it's an obsession, but I don't think that's necessarily a bad thing.

How would you characterise your management style?

I don't think you could characterise it, I think it's idiosyncratic. When you get knighted you go to the College of Arms to work out a motto and mine is perseverantia et celeritate, or "persistence and speed". I don't think business is like brain surgery, certainly not our business. The technology aspect is certainly demanding and not easy but having said that, that is where we are focused. I think speed is important. If I can't give an instant response it's because I am either unsure of the answer or I am worried about the impact of the answer. My father used to say "delay is a negative" and I think there's a lot in that.

Not that I am comparing our business to politics but I always remember somebody being asked "what's the difference between business and government?" and he said "every night Gordon Brown goes to sleep knowing there are three things that are going to happen tomorrow morning that he didn't know about when he went to bed". It's not on such a grand scale here but there is always good news and bad news. When you think of the scale of the operation it's hardly surprising really.

How do you account for your own success?

That's not for me to say, that's for others to say, it would be presumptuous for me to offer an opinion. My dad said "find a job you enjoy doing" and I think that's a critical component. It's a terrible phrase but "a bad decision on Monday is better than a good decision on Friday", meaning you should just get on with it and I think that's really important. It means if someone phones you, phone them back, if someone writes you a note, answer them as quick as you can because they have taken the trouble to write it, don't ignore them. Those are the sort of things that I think are important.

* *Preferred stock, similar to normal stock, represent a claim of ownership over a company, however any dividends due must be paid to preferred stock before normal stock (which can be in the form of a coupon rather than in relation to the size of profits. Preferred stock usually do not have voting rights on how the company is run. Convertible preferred includes an option for the holder to convert to common shares after a given date.*

Nick Park CBE

Creator, *Wallace & Gromit.*

"I always felt they had to be in pairs so Walter the Rat had a pet worm which was the victim really when it came to fishing".

Today Nick's feature films have multi-million pound budgets backed by some of the biggest names in Hollywood but his first characters were made of a product called Fuzzy Felt and inhabited a world based in his parents' backgarden. He began making films aged 13, mostly short sketches involving comedy duos such as Walter the Rat and a friendly worm, or Murphy and Bongo, a caveman and a dinosaur. Many filmmakers have had their first experiments in film at a young age but with Nick's work there is a noticeable continuity between some of the thinking behind the films he made in his teens and what became *Wallace & Gromit*. His father was the first to note the trademark humour in his short films and encouraged him to go to film school. A real lightbulb moment happened at a film festival where Nick had the idea of combining the kind of humour found in *Looney Tunes*, *Tom & Jerry* and Disney cartoons with plasticine animation.

Working with plasticine is a notoriously painstaking process. At Aardman Animations, the Bristol-based animation studio for *Wallace & Gromit,* the production teams rolled out roughly two minutes of footage every week, even when using 25-30 units of animators all working simultaneously. It's a process that Nick himself has found testing, the first *Wallace & Gromit* film, *A Grand Day Out*, which started as his graduation project, took seven years to complete. As well as having the stamina needed to work with clay, Nick is an obsessive character who never stops dreaming up new sketches, endlessly doodling on a notepad. Rarely in animation, or film in general, does so much of the creative work originate from one individual. As well as directing, writing and producing the *Wallace & Gromit*, *Chicken Run* and *Creature Comforts* films, much of the set design, "costume", accents, even the colour of the socks are mostly determined by Nick. He would be the first to say that animation is a collaborative effort, with ideas coming from many sections of the team at Aardman, but most of the core ideas come from Nick.

He was born and raised in Preston, Lancashire, where he attended Cuthbert Mayne High School. He is a graduate of Sheffield Polytechnic, now Sheffield Hallam University, and the National Film and Television School in Buckinghamshire. He is the recipient of four Academy Awards and five BAFTA Awards and until 2010 he had the rare accolade of winning an Academy Award in

131

every year he was nominated. He is also a recipient of the coveted gold *Blue Peter* badge.

You first picked up a camera at the age of 13, what were your first films about and how did you approach putting them together?

I was about 13 and my parents had this home movie camera that could do single frames. Art was the only thing that I was good at really and I could draw cartoons. I didn't know much about how to make animated cartoons and I found it quite hard to find out but my dad was a photographer and he told me some of the basic principles of how animation works and I turned some of my early cartoons into animations. I didn't have the technology to do cel animation like they do at Disney, so I went very low-tech. My first film used something called Fuzzy Felt. My mother is a dressmaker and she always had scraps of felt so I made my characters into felt cutouts and moved them on a board which was the background. I made up a story for a character called Walter the Rat and created The Rat and the Beanstalk. It took me a day to shoot. Which reminds me, I was quite obsessed with this Walter the Rat and I tried to do a drawn animation version which never came back from Kodak.

So there's a lost film somewhere! We'll have to get the BFI to chase it.

Yes we will! Because it didn't come back I tried something a bit quicker, using Fuzzy Felt. Then I tried something with puppets called Walter Goes Fishing. So I made half a dozen films just like that at home really.

I know the storylines weren't particularly deep at this stage but is there any noticeable continuity between the themes that we now see in the Aardman films, such as the humour, or the setting?

There probably is, I don't know in what way but the beginnings of what I did with plasticine did exist and I remember my dad picking up on the humour. That's what gave me a lot of confidence in the storytelling and the characters, that I could make people feel sad or make them laugh. I didn't realise this at the time but a lot of the characters I created were duos, like Wallace and Gromit. It comes from watching things like *Laurel & Hardy* and *Tom & Jerry*. I always felt they had to be in pairs so Walter the Rat had a pet worm which was the victim really when it came to fishing. I had another set of characters which no one has ever really seen called Murphy and Bongo, which was a caveman and a dinosaur character.

It's interesting how that has carried through. After school you

studied Communication Arts at Sheffield Polytechnic before going to the NFTS, a very elite film school, and then to Aardman Animations in Bristol who were mostly working on commercials. How did your career develop during those years to the point where you got involved with Aardman?

That's quite a long patch really but I'll try to sum it up. I always thought this would be a hobby really, forever, because coming from Preston in Lancashire, I had never heard of anyone going into the film business or TV so it wasn't on my radar as something I could do. I did a foundation art course at A-Level standard in Preston and there it was suggested by my dad that I should do a degree course in filmmaking. I went to Sheffield and made a couple of short films and with that applied to the National Film and Television School It was while I was there that I created *Wallace & Gromit,* which was my final year project. As it turned out it wasn't my final year project as it took me seven years in total to complete! I met Peter Lord and David Sproxton from Aardman during the course. They came and did a NFTS lecture one day and saw what I was doing and said, "why don't you come and help us on *Morph* over the summer?" Then they asked me to stay full-time but I kept telling them that I had this film to finish so they eventually said, "why don't you bring the film and we will negotiate with the film school and Aardman will help you finish it?"

That's an amazing opportunity.

Yes, it was, I was working on Aardman projects part-time so it was taking ages but it was great the way it worked out and I have stayed here ever since.

Where did the characters of Wallace and Gromit, particularly Wallace, come from? It must be connected with the duos you were working on in your early films?

Yes there were many inspirations. One of the reasons why I have gone for model animation, because I tried all sorts of techniques at college, was I just liked the way it was like a real film in that you use a camera, lighting and there's a physical set. I also loved comedy and cartoons so you get the best of both worlds. I tend to refer to my childhood a lot and things I remember from my parents' house or my granny's house. I often refer to things I saw, like the tea tray or the wallpaper, or the gnomes in my granny's garden and the shapes I remember as a kid which were attractive and interesting. The shape of the rocket in *A Grand Day Out* is influenced by cartoons like Tintin and films like H.G. Wells' *First Men in the Moon.* Wallace is said to be based on my dad but I discovered that in retrospect. I didn't consciously do it, it was after I made *A Grand Day Out* that I

Ashley Coates

remembered how my parents had made a caravan from scratch one year. My dad built it and seven of us went on holiday in it and my mum did the interior, with a cooker, a sink and wallpaper. So it was only after I made *A Grand Day Out* that I thought, "oh gosh I have made a film about my dad!"

One of the other interviewees for this series is Catherine Johnson, the writer of *Mamma Mia!*, who is also based in Bristol. She was telling me that she has lived a lifelong process of observing things, soaking stuff up from her friends or wondering around in public and it translates into a story later almost without realising. She's always thinking about stories and jotting ideas down, is that a similar scenario for you?

Definitely, always, you never switch off. I've always got a sketchbook handy and even if I'm watching TV or on the phone, I'm still doodling. My mum has always said that while I was a kid I was the quiet one, always observing, and I would love to go off drawing on my own, they were my happiest moments. She said I would stay on the phone and observe people, like Gromit, she would say.

Turning to *A Grand Day Out* again, you said some of that was inspired by your family both in terms of the characters and the setting, which is clearly Preston, the humour is in there as well. Did you just collect up all your ideas and go, "right I am just going to do what makes sense to me and like-it-or-lump-it as to whether anyone else will enjoy it"? Did you think about whether it would have wide appeal, because the risk would have been that it could have turned out quite narrow and eccentric? It turned out, of course, to be very popular.

It was partly the beauty of being at college really, that I was free from commercial pressures. I was always aware of audiences but to be honest from the beginning I have just wanted to make films that I would personally find entertaining and draw from all the things I loved when I was growing up. It was things like animations in kids' TV, Disney, *Laurel & Hardy*, Indiana Jones, European films, all mixed up. I've always wanted to make my own mark and when I started *A Grand Day Out*, I hadn't seen anything like it in that I hadn't seen a movie made with puppet animation or cartoon rules in a 3D world. I remember being at an animation festival and there were so many quiet, serious and obscure art films on but part of the festival was showing Chuck Jones' [*Looney Tunes* creator] films like Daffy Duck and Bugs Bunny which I really enjoyed and I came out thinking, "no one has ever done that kind of humour in clay animation, so that's what I am going to do". I do like audience reaction but it's hard to keep a perspective on what you are doing. If you're working on a feature that takes four or five years to complete and you think up some joke at the beginning, you then have to stick with it for the duration and you only see a reaction four or five years later, you can start loosing confidence in the jokes.

I suppose if you are spending so long on one project you can over-think it.

You start to question everything. The only people watching it while it's being made are the edit team and people working on the sound and they have all seen it a million times and half way through production no one is laughing any more. In the final mix you have seen the film about 300 times and everyone has stopped laughing, you start to think it may not be funny. I remember thinking that about *The Wrong Trousers*, thinking I wasn't sure what I had made. I wasn't sure if anyone would like it, quite honestly. I was quite bowled over when I went to the premiere and had the first reaction.

Thinking about the length of time it takes to produce these films, what are the mental effects of working with plasticine for so long. In the 1996 Australian current affairs programme, *60 Minutes*, you said working with plasticine might be compared to giving birth in terms of the pain of the process, is it just that 25 frames-per-second is tedious or are there other aspects to it that are tough?

The slowness is all part of it but it's also about being a bit of a perfectionist and finding it hard to let things go. I have worked with a wonderful team that understands this area really well so a lot of things are happening automatically now but I still like to be involved in every frame and every process from the storyboarding, to the design of the characters, I feel I know what colour the socks of every character should be. The bits I don't really know enough about are the music and sound effects, although obviously I am looking at them and approving them all the time. For a feature film, to get it done on schedule you are shooting a lot of scenes at the same time so it's all got to be storyboarded so you know where you are at any one time. It's quite a massive undertaking to keep an eye on it all.

When you do have a vision for what you want it to look like, as you've described, but you are working with a huge team of technicians, animators, and also pressure from finance and potentially America on some of your feature films, how do you keep creative control in that environment? Especially as you are on the quieter side personally and film is traditionally thought of as quite an aggressive industry.

135

I have done two feature films now, *Chicken Run* and *The Curse of the Were-rabbit*, there were massive learning curves both in terms of making full-length feature films and working with other studios, with Dreamworks. Jeffrey Katzenburg, from Dreamworks, had a huge appreciation for what we do here, I felt I was treated very well, I am not a person who naturally cracks the whip and refuses to come out of my trailer, though some of the plasticine models do. It was a learning curve but it was a case of learning where your real battles are, which battles to fight and which to leave. It was also important to know which areas they know a lot about, like the marketing and the music that will make it a big success in the cinema world. It was give and take really, with *Wallace & Gromit* it was easier because I had already made three shorts and I could say "Wallace would not do that". With those films we were trying to stay true to our own culture and sometimes the Americans wouldn't understand the accent or a turn of phrase so sometimes we had to compromise a little, but we pretty much dug our heals in.

Jim Henson said one of his main motivations was making as many people as possible happy. What would you say are your main motivations?

I think I would say I do like making people laugh but I also want to move them as well. I know it's comedy but I do want to make something meaningful, but I do see comedy as meaningful actually and being a great tonic. I think I want to tell a good story that makes people laugh and moves them.

The reaction that a lot of people have towards your films, particularly *Creature Comforts* and *Wallace & Gromit* is "oh, I wonder how they came up with that?". What is the development process like for one of your productions because I am guessing it is less formulaic than the approach you might take within a television production company or an ad agency in terms of how you go about creating new ideas?

At Aardman we pride ourselves on being original and not being formulaic, we do have to have a stamp of originality in it. We have a development team now and a number of different creatives and directors that are eager to make films. I personally feel kind of spoilt because I can mention an idea and everyone listens, I don't know how long it will last! Everything goes through some kind of evaluation and there are lots of ideas here that don't get taken up. If we are genuinely finding it funny then we hope other people will too. If you make it for yourself then that is how it will appeal to others but if you try hard to fit a perceived market you might miss badly.

Nigel Haywood CVO

Governor of the Falkland Islands
Consul-General, Basra 2009-10

*"The Argentine foreign minister went to the United Nations and told an astonished
audience about our top secret radar establishment, whereas it was in fact the University of
Leicester's array for detecting movement in the ionosphere".*

It's one of the most important roles in British diplomacy, overseeing the administration of a group of islands 8000 miles away in the South Atlantic. It's a role steeped in history, the first Governor took office in 1843, beginning of a period of continuous British oversight that was only interrupted in 1982 during the 74 days of Argentine occupation. Today the Governor has a very modern remit, set out in a series of continually updated acts of Parliament relating to the British Overseas Territories, but it is the tension with Argentina that still generates the greatest amount of attention in the islands.

Nigel's career in the Foreign Office began three years in the Army. He has since served in Israel, Lebanon, Iraq, Austria and Hungary. Between 2003 and 2008 he was UK Ambassador to Estonia and later Consul-General, Basra. He became Governor in 2010 as well as Commissioner for the South Georgia and South Sandwich Islands, a group of uninhabited islands in the South Atlantic with a total area of roughly 1,500 square miles. During his time on the Falkland Islands, provocations from Argentina's government, lead by Christina Fernandez, have often made headline news. The discovery of oil in the region, combined with the Argentine government's domestic troubles has made the sovereignty of the islands a central feature of President Fernandez's foreign policy. Fernandez maintains that British administration of the islands is a legacy of colonialism and has been pursuing bilateral negotiations through the UN as well as initiating a serious of confrontations with British officials. Even the Pope has been consulted over the Falklands when Fernandez made a visit to the Vatican in March 2013. The Foreign Office maintains that the islanders have chosen to be a British overseas territory and Argentina lost the right to discuss the sovereignty of the islands when the Argentine military junta invaded in 1982. 255 British soldiers and 649 Argentinians and three Falklands civilians lost their lives in the Falkland's War.

The Falkland Islands are an archipelago covering roughly 4,500 square miles, or about half the size of Wales. It has a permanent population of just under 3000 people, most of which are descendants of British settlers. There are two major islands, East and West Falkland, surrounded by 776 smaller islands. The Falklands, and the Falkland Sound, are named after Viscount Falkland, the Commissioner of the Admiralty who financed the 1690 expedition that accidentally discovered the islands. A succession of Spanish, Portuguese and French settlements were established on the islands which were temporarily abandoned by the British due to the demand on its military resources during the Napoleonic Wars. Today the Falklands are extremely well protected. At any one time, HMS Clyde, together with a frigate or a destroyer accompanied by a Royal Fleet Auxillary vessel are stationed in the region along with four Eurofighter Typhoons and a number of helicopters that are based on the islands themselves.

What was your route to the role of Governor?

Governorships are essentially Diplomatic Service jobs, although they can be advertised more widely. They come up in the same way that ambassadorships and high commissioner-ships come up. You leave a post at a particular time and you look at the jobs that are coming up in the next year and bid for those that attract you.

Was your specific path through the Diplomatic Service the kind of career you would expect for someone who goes on to be a Governor? Is there a typical path you can identify?

It's a very, very different job compared with being an ambassador or a head of any other post because you are head of the government, or at least you have a very defined role set out in the constitution. In preparing for that and then deciding whether or not to bid for the job you have to realise that a governorship is a very particular sort of role. Within the Diplomatic Service, normally your job is to represent the British government to whichever country you're in and try to persuade them to do things that they might not have realised are in their advantage to do. In a place like this you are responsible, in a very light-touch manner, to make sure that the show stays on the road. The crucial point about Overseas Territories is if something goes wrong within the territory, as in Montserrat or Tristan da Cunha, then the British government is going to have to pick up the bill.

The position of Governor of the Falkland Islands has existed since 1843, but has changed immensely since that time, what does the Governorship involve today?

There is part of it that is a straightforward figurehead role, for example, during the Liberation Day commemorations I turn up and take the salute at a parade wearing my uniform. On the other hand there is the close detailed work with members of the Legislative Assembly, and with the Chief Executive, on legislative priorities and on how best to take pieces of legislation forward. Within that, and I think this is true of any diplomatic or civil service job, you've got to get out and find out what people are thinking so that you don't work in a kind of vacuum. I spend as much time as I possibly can away from my desk.

Do you find that there are any conflicts between the more traditional, ceremonial aspects to the role and the modern straight-forwardly diplomatic parts of the job?

The constitution has been revised every ten years or so and I imagine will be revised in a few more years in an attempt to keep the relationship between the Governor and the territory up-to-date and as modern as possible. A long time ago this was a colony so it was run as a colony from the UK. Now the job is to help the economic, social and political development of the islands.

You are also Commissioner for another British Overseas Territory, the South Georgia and the South Sandwich Islands, what does this entail?

It's a very different job because there's no permanent population on the islands. There's a transitory group of about 30-40 people, consisting of scientists, museum staff, and the administrative staff for the islands, that are usually there at any given time. The government is effectively run from here. There's a room in this building [Government House] which has the main part of the South Georgia government in it, in addition to the offices that are down in South Georgia. Maintaining what is an absolutely outstanding area of natural beauty and scientific interest is our primary concern. We are encouraging tourism so that it can be part of the process of protecting the islands as it's easier to get appreciation for a territory worldwide if people can see it. The *Frozen Planet* series, a large part of which was filmed on South Georgia, has been extremely good publicity for it.

The islands probably aren't at the top of people's preferred holiday destinations but they have such a bleak and detached quality to them which must make them very refreshing places to be.

They are, it takes three or four days to get there as you can only get there by sea and when you arrive you really are away from it all. It's an absolute wildlife photographer's paradise.

It's not often noticed but the Falkland Islands are also areas of

incredible natural beauty, with 227 different species of bird and large breeding colonies of elephant and fur seals. But in the international sphere the islands tend to be seen primarily in the view of the diplomatic tensions with Argentina.

Yes and your underlying question is absolutely the right one, in the world's view we must position the islands away from being a source of dispute between the UK and Argentina towards something that's much more about the islands themselves. One of the projects we have been working very hard on is the establishment of a South Atlantic Environmental Research Institute down here which the Duke of Kent opened in November 2012. I recently spent a week on the East Coast of the United States talking to various universities about possible cooperation with us. Conservation is very high-up in people's minds on the islands and we are very good at it. But there is so much we simply don't know. Looking out of my window now at the harbour, you can go down and start shifting through the seaweed and find something that hasn't even been classified or at least no one knows much about. It's not just obvious things like penguins, whales, albatrosses and petrels, there's all sorts of less conspicuous species here.

Returning to your career, was it difficult moving away from the big cities you have been based in before to an island with a total population of around 3000 people.

There's a general point here about what the staff do within the Diplomatic Service. There are people who are fascinated by policy who want to spend all their time in London, Washington or Brussels, and the other main areas of policy formulation. There are others who are keen on the Arab world or the Far East. I've enjoyed postings that have a strong environmental element to them, so when I was in Budapest I got out of the city and spent a lot of time in the countryside. You have to use the standard unit of size when talking about countries which seems to be Wales, so Estonia is twice the size of Wales and with a population of only 1.3 million people, that was quite a small environment. I don't know why we talk about Wales, most people have no idea what you are talking about - but the Falklands are half the size of Wales.

Growing up in Cornwall was excellent preparation for coping in a small environment. I had to understand how easily you could mess up things in a small environment by getting interpersonal relationships wrong. You develop an instinct in those environments, for example, you might need to know that your grandmother borrowed somebody else's rolling pin in the 1920s and didn't give it back, therefore the two families aren't talking. I think it would be much more difficult to do this job if I came from a big city rather than Falmouth.

I always had the impression that the Diplomatic Service posts you wherever they want you but you seem to have been able to pick your own jobs?

When I was first in what was called personnel that era was just about coming to an end. Today, jobs are advertised and you apply for them. Jobs at a senior level are advertised throughout Whitehall so people from other departments can apply for them and some jobs are even advertised outside the service. You can pretty well pick your way through and I've been very lucky in being able to do that.

What would you say has been the most testing environment you have found yourself in during your career with the Foreign Office?

It's difficult to say, they are all testing in different ways, without sounding like the beginning of Anna Karenina. Basra is an obvious one, primarily because people were trying to kill you, there was the threat of rocks being thrown at you and if you went downtown there was always the threat of IEDs by the side of the road. Given that I was in charge of a team of 50 or so civilians then obviously I was concerned about their safety. I was also working very closely with British forces because there was always a linkage between what you as a civilian were trying to do and what the military was trying to do. It was very helpful that I had spent three years in the army as I wouldn't have had a clue what they were talking about otherwise.

Were there any particularly disturbing moments when you were in Basra?

No, I don't think so because when UK forces were in the area there were extremely good rocket batteries. As soon as the alarm went off you dived under your desk and sensible people had cushions, books and cans of Coke in case the alert went on for a long time. You had to be pretty unlucky to get hit as we took a lot of precautions.

Living 8000 miles away, the perspective of most Britons to the Argentine claim on the islands is inevitably quite different to anyone who is living on the Falklands, how have you approached the Argentinian issue?

The important thing about the Argentine position that the world needs to understand is it is a fundamentally flawed one. I think the most important task has been to get the elected representatives of the islanders to travel around the world and set out exactly what the situation really is on the Falklands. Argentina benefitted from an information vacuum for too long a period from which they were able to get out a lot of spurious, misleading and downright untruthful statements about the history of the islands and the current situation. When I got here the most obvious thing to do from my perspective was to get information out there, using the diplomatic network to help, and encouraging people to go out and get the message across. We understand that there is a regional imperative for other countries to show solidarity with Argentina but so long as they do so knowing what they are signing up to is not true. Speaking to politicians in Latin America and elsewhere many are quite surprised when they find out what has really been going on here. The great advantage of our position is that it is backed up by evidence, a lot of which is in Argentine archives, rather than their position which is made up.

You've talked about the information side, how much does military posturing play into the situation?

Argentina has decided that one of the things it is going to convince the world is that we are militarising the South Atlantic. It makes up some utterly wonderous stuff on this front, for example, the Argentine foreign minister went to the United Nations and told an astonished audience about our top secret radar establishment, whereas that is in fact the University of Leicester's array for detecting movement in the ionosphere. There are other examples, such as their suggestions that our missiles might reach Brazil whereas they have a range of about seven miles and are anti-aircraft missiles anyway. That said, we do have a military presence here, it is designed to deter any potential aggressors. It is at the minimal level required to provide the defence that is necessary and it wouldn't be necessary at all if Argentina hadn't invaded in 1982. There was very little in the way of forces before then and we have learnt our lesson.

Sir Peter Bazalgette

Television Entrepreneur

"When people say, "I've been lucky" or "you've been lucky" I always think to myself, "people make their luck".

Over the last 15 years, Peter Bazalgette has brought some of the best known television formats to our screens. He founded his own production company, Bazal, in the early 90s, making the most of the experience he built up at the BBC as a producer. He is responsible for the creation of some of the most important entertainment shows in recent television history, including *Ready Steady Cook, Changing Rooms* and *Ground Force*. Crucially, these programmes were not only popular in the UK, but many were sold abroad, in as many as 30 countries. Peter is perhaps best known as the man that brought *Big Brother* to the UK, starting a ten year long craze that dominated the news as much as it dominated Channel 4's evening schedule. The popularity of the series has been a major factor in the success of Endemol, the international production company that absorbed Bazal in the early 90s. During his time as the Chair of Endemol UK and Creative Director of the Endemol Group, the value of the firm trebled to €3.2 billion.

Remarkably Peter barely watched television for the first 12 years of his life, as his parents never bought one. He grew up in London and joined the BBC as a news trainee after graduating from Cambridge with a third in law. A university friend, Jon Makinson, now chairman of Penguin and the National Theatre, has described him as a "superstar of the [Cambridge] union. His trademark qualities are that he manages to be both irreverent and self-deprecating on the one hand, and yet serious and thoughtful on the other, all features that were well in evidence in his Cambridge days". As of January 2013, Peter has been Chair of the Arts Council England. He has served on a number of boards at major media organisations including ITV, the Royal Television Society, the English National Opera and the Department for Culture, Media and Sport.

Let's start with Cambridge. You were President of the very prestigious Cambridge Union, whose speakers have included Winston Churchill and Ronald Reagan, but you left with a third.

Actually I very nearly didn't get into university at all for that matter! My contemporaries are all about two or three years younger than me. I had reasonable A-Levels, I don't know how I managed to ruin my entrance to universities but everyone turned me down the first time round. So then I went off and taught in a school for a year before getting into Cambridge, not to the college I applied for but to another college which gave me an interview on the 13th hour. I got a poor degree because I spent all my time running the Union.

Were you one of those students who allowed their co-curricular activities to consume all their energies?

In those days it was a very liberal regime, if you were doing lots of stuff they didn't come and beat you up because you weren't taking your work seriously. My son is at Cambridge at the moment and it's very different today, they take how hard you are working very seriously and keep a close eye on you. In my day there was an amused tolerance. I ran the Union and I did some student journalism and had a great time. To be honest I was lucky to get a third, so it's not a good example to anyone, least of all my son!

But the experience was probably more useful than if you had buried your head in books?

Yes and having done student journalism and been involved in the politics of the university, when I applied to be a BBC news trainee, I had a pretty good idea of journalism as an industry and a good understanding of politics.

They must have been aware of what the Cambridge Union is and what your role there would have involved.

Yes today though I don't think they would have given me a job if they knew I got a third. Back then they didn't seem to care what the degree was but people are much more concerned by the quality of the degree today, quite rightly too.

You joined the BBC's graduate news scheme before becoming a researcher, working with Ester Ranzten for a while before progressing to being a producer, working on *Food & Drink* amongst other programmes. Apart from gaining an understanding of the production environment, what was it that led you to starting your own company and working on your own formats? Were you thinking "I can do this better"?

I toyed with a bit of presenting but really I was acting as a producer and an assistant producer, or researcher. I specialised in programmes like *That's Life*, which was a bit like a local newspaper on national television and it had funny items and human interest stories but it also had some quite hard consumer stories as well and it was a way of making factual information entertaining. It was a very, very formative experience working with Ester Ranzten on that programme because it gave me an interest in how can we make information entertaining. Everything I did not long afterwards in the 90s with *Ready Steady Cook* and *Ground Force* was about taking stuff that people wanted information on and making it more entertaining and creating a bigger audience for it. So that was a desire to entertain and to inform.

The other aspect I would point out from an entrepreneurial point-of-view is that those of us who had about ten years experience were therefore getting into our 30s when a big opportunity arose, which was the emergence of the independent production sector. TV was once solely in the hands of the BBC and ITV and not only were the channels in their hands but all the production was in-house. There was no diversified, competitive, content industry. Margaret Thatcher's government had brought in Channel 4 in the 80s which was only allowed to commission from independent producers, and that really created the independent sector. Then in 1988 they brought in another rule which meant the BBC and ITV would have to commission from independent producers, thus liberalising this very valuable asset called the broadcasting spectrum. What it meant in the 80s was those of us that had enough experience had an opportunity to capitalise on it. When broadcasting liberalised I happened to be there and I happened to be the right age.

What was the process like for creating hit shows like *Changing Rooms* and *Ready Steady Cook* for example? Where did those ideas come from and how much did you rely on data to inform the development process?

If you're creating hit shows there are one or two pretty important provocations to make it happen. One is that you get a brilliant brief, and there were a couple of people running the channels at the BBC in those days who were very clever. I called them "cool hunters", by which I mean they were able to sniff the wind and say "I think we ought to have a primetime programme about DIY and interiors". This was when B&Q, garden centres and Ikea were taking off and people had more money to spend improving their homes and magazines covering the subject were proliferating. Then they said to people like me, humble producers, "I think we need to have a programme about this" and without having had that call a producer probably wouldn't go off and invent the show.

So that is number one, a very intelligent and provocative brief. Number two, extreme pressure! Let me give you an example, for *Changing Rooms*, the guy running BBC2 had said, "you've got to come up with a show about DIY and interiors, can you make it entertaining, like *Ready Steady Cook?*". I got on a train at Tottenham Court Road in Central London and I was traveling to Television Centre in West London and I turned to my producer and said, "this idea sucks doesn't it?!" She agreed that it wasn't very good so I said, "we have eight stops to think of another idea", and at Holland Park, which was two-thirds of the way there I said, more in desperation than anything else, "what would it be like if two neighbours swapped houses and did up rooms in each others' houses?" So we pitched it and it went down very well and got commissioned.

You mentioned data and market research, that feeds into the brief in the first place and it can inform the creative process. Before we produced *Ground Force*, gardening had never had more than three million viewers on BBC2. *Ground Force* ended up with twelve million viewers on BBC1 and that was informed by the fact that we saw some research which informed us that young people were treating their gardens like they were treating their interiors. They weren't willing to plant some seeds and wait six months and learn how to garden. People wanted instant makeovers of gardens. Then in the creative process you need the right people as well, you need the right cast and crew.

You said somewhere that television has a lot to learn from advertising, in terms of the origination of creative ideas, what did you mean?

Advertising lives or dies by the quality of its ideas. It is organised for creativity which is why they have creative directors, I was the first person in TV to call myself a creative director and I was trying to steal their way of working. They have a very organised system where they have creative briefs and planners, who define that brief before it goes to the creatives who come up with a creative solution. That is what you need for TV too.

Big Brother was already a successful format in the Netherlands before you brought it to the UK, and then rolled it out internationally. What were you trying to achieve with the programme in the UK and what adjustments did you need to make to the format to make it the success that it became?

Probably two things and in this we had the help of Channel 4 as well. Point one, we needed to make it more intense and point two, we had to make it more cool. The Dutch format only had an expulsion every two weeks and the Director of Programming at Channel 4 decided we needed an expulsion every week which is what lead to the Friday night big event, so that was a very shrewd observation of Channel 4's, rather than our own. In terms of making it more cool, much of this was aesthetic. The whole design and feel of the Dutch show made it look a bit like a 1970s light entertainment show so our producers revamped the setting, Elementfour came up with this iconic theme tune for it, and it was given the eye for the logo. The Dutch wanted to stop us doing it as they thought the show should be done exactly in their format everywhere around the world. That's how *Who Wants To Be A Millionaire?* had worked, the same studio, same layout, same lighting everywhere around the world. I'm afraid we subverted that.

This is a more introspective question and you don't have to answer it if you don't want to but how do you account for your own success?

I think the number one point would be *carpe diem* [seize the day], it's seizing opportunities. When people say, "I've been lucky" or "you've been lucky" I always think to myself, "people make their luck". I had no idea what I was going to do and I had no idea what direction it was going to go in but I do feel at several points I seized opportunities. I seized an opportunity to join the BBC and seized the opportunity to set up my own production company. You don't have to have a grand plan but you do have to have the balls to seize opportunities.

What would you say to someone who is starting out in the creative industries?

I would say that, compared to when I got into it, it's much more liberalised and freelance. That's a good and a bad thing, the bad part of it is, there isn't a career structure like there used to be when there were two or three large companies. The good side to this is that there are many more opportunities for you to decide your own destiny and jump about and do different things. There is more opportunity to do what you want to do because you are not entering a big bureaucratic entity, which you would have entered into in my day. But the main point I would make is that because it's liberalised, you will succeed if you are determined enough but only if you are determined enough. You will have to knock doors down, you will have to send out 100 emails, you will have to analyse the marketplace and you may have to work as a runner. It does require you to grit your teeth but don't get depressed because if you do try hard enough you will succeed.

Rob Law MBE

Founder, Trunki.

"I just got on with it".

Having been laughed off *Dragons' Den* in an episode called "Wheelie Rubbish", Rob Law's luggage business has gone from strength to strength. Two years after his 2006 disaster in the den, Trunkis were selling at the rate of one every 3.5 minutes but it was a hard won victory. Rob entered *Dragon's Den* optimistic that an investment from one of the entrepreneurs could turn his fortunes around but he left thinking he had ruined his business. In a memorable scene, Theo Paphitis snapped a piece off Trixi, the "female" Trunki and Deborah Meaden declared that there was no market for the case. Having aimed for a £100,000 investment for 10% of his business, Rob left with nothing.

Rob came up with the idea for Trunki while he was a student at Northumbria University. It was when he was researching for a university competition that he found the range of children's luggage available uninspiring and set about designing his own solution. Rodeo, as it was then known, was born but it would take several years for it to enter the market, during which time Rob worked as a product designer for a number of major brands. In 2003, the first Trunkis began to be produced under a licensing relationship with a Chinese firm. It was unable to produce a marketable product and went into liquidation in 2005. Unexpectedly the publicity Rob gained from the den caught the attention of a number of retailers that declared their interest in the product. By August 2008, over 120,000 Trunkis had been sold worldwide in 22 countries and they were becoming a ubiquitous presence at airports in the UK.

What did you study at school?

I did Design, Physics and Maths at A-Level. At university I did Design for Industry which included product design.

Did you have a clear idea of where that might take you at that stage?

Yes, when I was fourteen I did work experience for a design consultancy and that's where I decided I wanted to be a product designer. I went off and did the relevant qualifications and A-Levels I needed.

The idea for Trunki was born out of your university experience and it hummed away in the background for nine years. Were you happy working professionally or were you thinking "oh I should be pursuing this"?

I put it away for a couple of years while I worked in Taiwan and Australia. I worked in many parts of the world as a product design consultant. It was when I was going up the East Coast of Australia in a camper van meeting people who didn't seem to know what to do with their lives, that I worked out exactly what I wanted to do, I wanted to be a product designer. I ended up developing the idea for a ride-on suitcase that I had at university a lot further while I was traveling. I have actually got sketches on the back of American Express letter-headed paper from when I was doing some temping work.

Did they not notice?

I was on the phone so I was just sketching away. Then when I came back in 2002 I approached the Prince's Trust to help me get the business sorted.

What did the Prince's Trust do for you at that stage?

I was living with my parents up in Chester so it was the Chester branch and I approached them just for some help really, just to try and get a bit of cash to get the business off the ground and get some advice. They helped me figure out the business plan which was to license the product to a manufacturer, it wasn't to start up on my own.

That was quite a risky move for you, moving out of the licensing arrangement and starting Magmatic and doing it yourself.

Magmatic was first started for the licensing arrangement and that was in 2003. I licensed the design to a toy company at the beginning of 2003 and my entire £4000 Prince's Trust loan went on solicitor fees drawing up the contract, so we use the solicitors very frugally these days. There was a license deal for three years which finished when the company, the licensee, went into liquidation. Then I decided, having worked in Bristol quite a few times for some FMCG [fast-moving consumer goods] brands that I was getting a bit bored of being a product designer. I thought what Trunki really needed was a really strong big brand behind it, the company I licensed it to they had sold us a cheap toy and they hadn't sold us a lifestyle product.

Who were you working for before?

A company called Kinneir Dufort in Bristol.

What was there client base like?

I was managing a lot of Unilever work, so I was working with Lynx, Dove, Domestos, Persil, other projects for Durex. God, who else did I work with? M&Ms and Maltesers.

Did that help you focus in terms of how you would go about working independently?

Not working independently but more about getting the brand, messaging and marketing right.

Was it a struggle getting yourself organised once you had chosen to work for yourself?

My previous employer was very flexible and they let me take a day off a week to investigate the business plan and it wasn't until the first stock arrived on 5th May 2006 that I could actually quit, having a basic income stream from the website sales and small independents.

In 2006, a lot of people watched as Theo Paphitis broke "Trixxie", your pink Trunki. How big a set back did failure in the *Dragons' Den* prove to be?

The exposure in the end turned into a phenomenal bit of marketing for us and I wouldn't change a thing but at the time I left the den thinking I had ruined my business. The BBC advertised the episode as "Wheelie Rubbish" and it was a setback but I'd had a factory go bust in China where we had to rescue the tooling out and I'd had quite a few other setbacks such as the hand luggage ban in 2006, so I was used to getting a few knocks.

What drove you to continue?

I guess they never really knocked me down, you just carry on, keep trying to get it past that hurdle. It never really phased me too much, I just got on with it.

What do you say when you meet the dragons now, because you must encounter them every now and then?

Yes, I tend to bump into them at big functions.

What is the sort of feedback you get from them because Duncan Bannatyne came out saying that you were the "one that got away".

He did but then he changed his mind and came out on Twitter saying that I was the worst possible figurehead for British business. I think he was on a bit of a bad day and he wanted to see our company accounts and we said he would have to wait until they are on Company's House.

But generally I guess the feedback is a little more warm.

Yes I suppose the most poignant was from a few years ago when I went to pick up the Growing Business Award from New Product Company of the Year. Theo Paphitis was presenting the awards so I passed him on the steps on the way down the stage as I was going up to get my award.

What would your advice be to people who have got a product, or think they've got a product, and want to go out and sell something?

You've got to go in with your eyes wide open, if it was easy, everyone would be doing it. I get contacted daily by inventors who think they've got a great idea but actually it's an idea they think is great and no-one else does. Rule number one is to get your market research done and make sure that your target market think it's a good idea and figure out what price they are prepared to pay for it. If you have a brilliant idea that costs ten times more than what anyone is willing to pay, it's a dead end. Also if you are up and running in business then you are going to get a few set backs and knocks. It's a challenging environment but you've got to keep on being very driven and determined and that's why most entrepreneurs who succeed are that kind of person.

What sort of things do people propose to you as business ideas?

We've got all sorts, we normally sign NDAs [Non Disclosure Agreements] with them, but things like a device for making sure your caravan is level through to various nursery products.

What are they expecting you to do with them?

Well if it fits our target market which is children's travel products then we're interested to hear more, so say out of a hundred ideas maybe ten fit that category, then we will find out a little bit more and offer some advice to go and do some research. Maybe three will come back and only one we'll look at. We've looked seriously at about four or five designs and ended up taking three.

The odds of getting it to market aren't favourable.

You could almost say that about five hundred inventors have contacted us and we've ended up taking three. That's the success rate for a product really. We treat rough ideas all the time with my design background and my design team and it really is a hundred-to-one rule, you've got to have one hundred ideas to come up with one excellent one. We've now got a line of six product lines and each one of those has come from a massive array of ideas we've looked at over time.

Is there anything you can highlight in particular that you have learnt from being a business owner as opposed to working professionally?

The biggest thing I have learnt from where I stand now is I've got a really good holistic view of the whole supply chain process from coming up with an idea, and knowing that process through to understanding manufacturing technologies and techniques to reduce price, through to the logistics of how much it costs to ship stuff and trying to get as much onto pallets and containers as possible, making things durable for shipping, all the way through to what it looks like on the shop shelf. Then you've got to factor in all the safety standards, and understanding those, and that parents and children want to find those products desirable so its a huge thing to take on.

So what's been the highlight of your entrepreneurial career so far?

There's been quite a few but I suppose getting an MBE from the Queen was quite a big one, winning SME of the Year at the National Business Awards this year, I could probably give you one per year actually!

Would you go about doing anything differently if you were to attempt the same work again?

I think you learn a lot from your mistakes so if you don't make them earlier on then you may make even bigger ones later so I'm a big fan of saying "I wouldn't change a thing", life's a learning process and it certainly is in business. There are things I may think I could have done differently but if I hadn't done them I might not have learnt from those mistakes.

Ashley Coates

Rowan Williams PC FBA FRSL
(Lord Williams of Oystermouth)

Archbishop of Canterbury 2002-2012
Master of Magdelene College, Cambridge, 2013-

"I have seen people holding onto their faith in nightmare circumstances, making something of it and making their lives richer. If they can do it, perhaps some other people can".

Born to a Welsh-speaking family in Swansea, Rowan Williams went to a nearby state-school where he proved himself to be a relentlessly studious child. By his early-teens he was not only reading extensively but also writing poetry and essays on history and religion. He went on to study and teach theology at both Oxford and Cambridge. In 1986 he became the youngest professor at Oxford, a year after having been arrested for protesting against nuclear proliferation at RAF Alconbury. Following a series of academic appointments he was elected and consecrated as Bishop of Monmouth, in a "calling he could not refuse", giving him an opportunity to return to the Church in his home country. He later became Archbishop of Wales before taking up the See of Canterbury. Rowan was the 105th Archbishop in a line that goes back more than 1500 years to Augustine of Canterbury in 597. His appointment was unconventional on a number of levels. He was the youngest Archbishop in 200 years and the first bishop from outside the Church of England chosen to be Archbishop of Canterbury in over 500 years. His background as an academic, rather than a "career priest", also contrasted with his predecessors.

He became Archbishop during a time of division, uncertainty and worry within the Church of England about where it was heading as an institution. Issues such as the ordination of women bishops, gay marriage and the decline of Sunday Church attendance were among some of the more pressing concerns for Lord Williams when he took on the job. A former Bishop of Oxford told him, "God has given you all the gifts and, as your punishment, he has made you Archbishop of Canterbury." Lord Williams made considerable headway in dealing with some of the Church's most divisive issues as well as expanding their development work abroad.

You grew up in Swansea and went to Dynevor, a nearby state school. How would you characterise your upbringing at home and at school?

155

My parents originated in the Swansea Valley, in an industrial village. My father came from a mining family and my mother came from a farming family. I was an only child and it was a home where there was a lot of encouragement for doing well at school. School itself, although not at all a very spectacular building or a well-known school, was incredibly encouraging and very warm and a pleasing place to be.

You started reading complex material and writing quite extensively from a very early age. What do you think was compelling you to do that?

Apart from the obvious answer that I was showing off! We were encouraged to write and I can remember one essay I was asked to write when I was about 15, and suddenly thinking, "gosh there are ideas here which are worth working out on paper". I was driven to look into it by a teacher.

Your path to senior cleric roles was very unconventional, was it always your intention for your academic career to translate into a career within the Church?

I suppose right from the start of my teaching of theology I saw it as something I was doing for the Church. I wanted to help increase my understanding, and other people's understanding of the Church, about where we were and what we were up to. I have always said that what I would like to see is a learning Church, a Church that is willing to ask questions and explore and grow. I saw my teaching as very rooted in that. From the very first time I was teaching in Cambridge, I was going out quite a bit to do study days with clergy, weekend parishes and that sort of thing.

What were the major themes that interested you during the strictly academic phase of your career?

Two themes really engaged me. One was a better understanding of how people pray and what the theological background is to that and the other theme was what theology has to say about contemporary social and political questions. I had always been fairly involved in social and political issues while I was a student and afterwards. Some people might say that it's two extremes, being very world-engaged but also thinking a lot about contemplation and solitude. To me, a figure like Thomas Merton, one of the great religious writers, of the 50s and 60s, was an enormous inspiration. He was a monk who wrote a great deal about the spiritual life and also wrote a great deal about the issues of race and war in America.

Were you at all concerned that by moving into a demanding ecclesiastical role, thinking particularly about becoming Bishop of Monmouth, that you were going to loose the opportunity to work on your writing?

There was an inevitable price to pay, I couldn't do the same kind of scholarship as I had done before. That was just something that had to be budgeted-in. The call to be Bishop of Monmouth was something I felt I couldn't say no to. Here I was being asked to go back to my native country and serve the Church. I had always said that I wanted to put what I had at the disposal of the Church and they took me at my word. I didn't feel a moment's regret about that, not a moment.

On the topic of contemplation and solitude, Christianity offers many means by which an individual can reflect and self-evaluate, such as prayer and meditation. What do you do to help you clear your mind?

It's absolutely essential to have a serious period of silence every day. I have always tried to maintain that but as part of a regular pattern. I start the day with a substantial period of silence, I go on a retreat or two every year, going away for a few days for silence and reflection. It's also useful to have a habit of praying during the day, getting into the habit of stopping ever so often and concentrate your energies a bit.

It helps you maintain focus.

That's the idea, yes. Trying to remember what matters and what doesn't, which I don't always succeed with.

Am I right in saying that you were arrested for singing psalms outside a US military base?

I'm afraid you are yes.

How did that come about?

This was about 1985 and I was part of Christian CND [Campaign for Nuclear Disarmament]. At that time there was a great deal of anxiety about the proliferation of American nuclear missiles in British bases and some of us at Christian CND just decided to go up to the air force base at Alconbury and say some prayers. It was Ash Wednesday, the day when Lent begins, so we start to

157

think about repentance and say some prayers. So we climbed over the fence and said some prayers. Fortunately they couldn't work out exactly what to charge us with as we hadn't cut the wires and we thought quite hard about doing it in a way that would mean we couldn't be charged with anything.

Was that your only act of political protest or were you part of other demonstrations for the CND movement?

I was regularly at CND meetings and rallies and spoke to various groups over the years. When I was a bishop in Wales I was quite actively involved in protests over the closure of the mines in the early 90s. I had some very inspiring contact with the people that rescued Tower Colliery, the pit having been closed was taken over by the miners themselves as a workers cooperative that ran for many years very successfully.

The Archbishop of Canterbury has an almost overwhelming number of responsibilities, ranging from the ceremonial to the administrative. It looks like a Chairman, CEO and Chief Operating Officer all rolled into one. There are the responsibilities to Diocese of Canterbury, the Province of Canterbury, overseeing Anglican communities and an array of other official roles within academic institutions in England, such as trusteeships and governorships. Where did you dedicate most of your time and to what extent did you feel distracted by some of the less substantive requirements of the role?

There always seemed to be meetings to chair but quite a lot of the work, like getting out into parishes and to schools and so forth I enjoyed greatly. It was a great regime for me, I loved school visits and as far as I possibly could I used to try to get to a parish at least once every Sunday. I was able to get around parishes in Kent when I was Archbishop. The international trips were often very exhausting but they also provided huge inspiration. Going to somewhere like the Congo or Sudan, or Pakistan, you see a Church very much under pressure, doing extraordinary things.

The political side of the Church, or rather the issues-orientated side of the Church, is that something you are keen to see more of?

It's certainly not the only thing the Church is for, the Church is there to help people be holy and loving. One of the ways we express that holiness and love is through the way we serve one another and my interest in international development has grown considerably. What could we do to help a village in

Kenya or a church-school in central Sudan? How do you best support and encourage people who are doing that very basic, hands-on work? Part of my work for the last few years was trying to establish a better network for aid, relief and development agencies in the Anglican community. We needed more sharing of resources, experiences and training and I think we ended up with quite a robust network in the end.

The Church has encountered a number of highly divisive issues over the last decade, what would you say was your greatest challenge as Archbishop?

The obvious answer is that I was Archbishop during a period of enormous international tension between the various parts of the Anglican family. The great challenge was trying to get people to talk to one another and broker relationships, which is usually a recipe for being unpopular with everybody.

Politically, was your situation not unlike that of the recent Coalition in that you were often caught between parts of the Christian community that we might call more liberal and the more Orthodox community and the need to juggle the interests on both sides?

It's not at all a simple stand-off. On both sides there are people of real integrity and real stature. The lines of division don't always run where you think they would. It required quite a bit of diplomacy, some hard conversations and certainly required what I talked about earlier, the process by which you sit down and remind yourself what it's all about.

What would you say is your greatest achievement?

I never know how to answer that because it's too early to say. Two projects I worked on during my time as Archbishop that seem to have gathered traction are the efforts to get a proper international network for development and the innovative missionary programme I tried to launch when I first became Archbishop. The programme is about trying to get Christian communities started away from the mainstream church, not necessarily meeting on Sundays or meeting in Church buildings. Over the years we reckon that we reached something like 30,000 people with that programme. Although the statistics for Sunday worship are not all that encouraging, the fact is that on the one hand the rate of decline has definitely leveled off, and on the other, Sunday attendance no longer measures people's involvement with the Church in quite the way it used to. I do feel quite pleased about how that turned out and I had fantastic staff and colleagues who helped to take that forward.

After you stood down you spoke of having "unfinished business" within the Church, what would you most like to have done if your tenure could have continued?

I would have been, very, very happy if I could have left with the issue of the ordination of women bishops settled. Last year was very hard, I had hoped when I first announced that I would be standing down that this particular cycle would be over. I think I was too optimistic.

There was a lot of movement though.

Yes but I think last November [2012] was a bitter blow for all sorts of people.

Over the years you have spoken to many prominent atheists, including Richard Dawkins. Which aspect of your faith, rather than the position of the Church, have you been challenged on the most?

The one challenge that keeps coming back, and to which there is never a cut-and-dried answer, is the question of suffering. I remember when Jon Humphrys asked me directly to answer his questions on the *Today* programme the morning after the killing of children in Beslan [Russia] some years ago. It was very tough and it's the question that people find the most difficult. How could you talk about a God of love when etc etc? The theoretical answers are often not of much use to people. All I can say is I have seen people holding onto their faith in nightmare circumstances, making something of it and making their lives richer. If they can do it, perhaps some other people can.

Sergeant Ryan McCready

First Battalion, Royal Irish Regiment
"Most Outstanding Soldier", 2011 Military Awards.

"Both times I was hit, the dust settled and nothing had changed, we were still in the same place, we were still fighting for our lives and the enemy was still fighting with us".

Being relocated by your employer is a massive upheaval for anyone but it is certainly a shock to the system when your next position is in a small Afghan village in Southern Helmand. Two weeks into his first deployment to Afghanistan in 2008, then Corporal McCready stepped on an initiator for an improvised explosive device (IED) causing extensive damage but sparing them their lives. On his moste recent deployment Sergeant McCready was injured during a day skirmishing with the Taliban. He was leading a platoon pursuing enemy fighters when an intense firefight erupted and Sergeant McCready was his with an enemy rocket propelled grenade. Despite his hardship, Sergeant McCready continued to serve with intelligence and bravery, earning him the Most Outstanding Soldier award at the 2011 "Millies". Presenting the award to Sergeant McCready, Prince William said: "You exemplify to an extraordinary degree the unique qualities that make the British soldier second to none - courage, steadfastness, professionalism, sense of humour and a deep humanity".

On arriving for McCready's interview at RMA Sandhurst, the academy's protocol officer, Lieutenant Colonel Roy Parkinson, pointed out a stained-glass window of a Victorian soldier fighting in Afghanistan, a reminder that the British had been involved in major conflicts in Afghanistan three times before. The first Anglo-Afghan War started in 1839 and lasted until 1842, taking the lives of 4500 British and Indian soldiers. The second began in 1878, and a final conflict ended in 1919. Many of the difficulties of fighting in the region remain the same; a linguistic and cultural gulf between both the combatants and the local people, the terrain, which is arid, mountainous, vast and mostly lawless and an enemy that is driven not by attachment to a particular nationality but by dogmatic ideology. Success in Helmand required the full range of skills demanded by modern warfare. Alongside the complex combat operations, there was a huge emphasis on understanding and winning the loyalty of the local people. One of the reasons for McCready's recognition at the Military Awards was his ability to foster goodwill amongst the Afghans, who, his superiors noted, held him in especially high regard.

Born and raised in County Londonderry, Ireland, Ryan McCready enlisted in the Army straight after his GCSEs. A hint of his future abilities came when he was awarded the accolade of "Best Recruit" out of the 130 men in his intake at the Catterack Infantry Training Centre. He was too young to serve in the invasion of Iraq in 2003 but from 2005 he took part in Force Protection for vessels moving through the most dangerous parts of the region. He describes his time in Afghanistan as constructive but a huge learning curve that pushed him to the edge of his abilities.

There are many reasons why people choose to join the armed forces, what drew you to the Army?

I was fairly young when I was first exposed to the Army because I had grown up in County Londonderry in Northern Ireland. It was during the latter end of The Troubles so it was a normal thing to see soldiers patrolling the streets with weapons and camouflage and stopping cars at checkpoints and so on. The thought I had was, "I want to be there, I want to stand there with a weapon and do something positive and have impact wherever I go". Initially that was the attraction, the uniformity and the weapons systems, they could pretty much do anything, I don't mean they could do anything that they wanted to, but there was always an expression that with the Army, there was nothing they couldn't move. Towards the end of my school time, when I was 16 and I had done a lot more research, decided to join the infantry. I thought if I am going to join the Army, I want to be at the tip of the spear and I want to be the first in the door, or out of the door if it's an aircraft. It really was a strong drive and there was nothing else in contention with it.

We're used to seeing images, some of the quite vivid, from conflicts in the Middle East, showing the effects of roadside bombs. The footage from helmet cameras shown on the news and in documentaries like *Our War* have given a huge audience a sense of what it can be like to be in the field. What would you say was your most frightening moment in Afghanistan?

It's hard to pinpoint the most frightening moments because we are trained to deal with the most frightening moments from day one when we join the Army but nonetheless you still get your moments. On my first deployment to Afghanistan, I stepped on a pressure-plate IED, which was connected to three anti-personnel mines. However, I was lucky and I stepped on the initiator, with no high explosives underneath it, it was a daisy chain to my rear with around three to four metres circumference, so the guy behind me took the majority of the blast and I got thrown forward, and that was maybe 2-3 weeks into my deployment in Afghanistan. It was a major wake up call that things are real and there's no second chances. Luckily, we both survived, he had minor shrapnel, I had minor concussion. More recently, in Afghanistan, I got hit by a grenade from a rocket propelled grenade from an under-slung grenade launcher, the blast was fairly close and most of the shrapnel hit me on the left-hand side of my body. I sustained blast and shrapnel to my face, neck and arm. Both times I was hit, the dust settled and nothing had changed, we were still in the same place, we were still fighting for our lives and the enemy was still fighting with us.

How do you discipline yourself into not letting those events effect you, I realise part of it is training but it is one thing knowing that an IED explosion is possible and another to actually experience it and carry on. How do you deal with fear?

I think we must have fear, I think there is always an element of fear there which gives us good judgement, or at least moral judgement, when it comes to our risk versus reward in those environments. I would probably put it down to the suppression of fear with our objectives and our mission. The way our training goes is that our mission comes first and we come a close second and if we push hard, be it against the enemy or the environment then we will push through and we will survive. I would probably break it into two parts, one is the threat itself, which is always on your mind, secondly you've got the fear of that threat actually following through. So being on patrol every single day, three times a day. in high threat areas for IEDs which have been placed, or indeed being susceptible to small arms fire, that is a constant threat and a key factor that you have to consider.

So it is in the background?

We are comfortable working in chaos, so it becomes normal, you allow it to become normal so that you can operate in that environment, or situation. On the other hand sometimes the actual threat follows through and the impact of what has happened creates a new situation, then it is a different dynamic and the way we react, it's done in drills so initially the drill happens without thinking, whether that be taking cover from enemy fire or attending a bloodied casualty. Once the drill is completed you can take a step back, take a moment to absorb the atmosphere and develop a workable plan.

A major focus of your operations was winning the trust of the local people in Zarghun Kalay, perhaps the most intellectually challenging part of your mission and one of the areas you were recognised for at the Millies. How did you go about

That was one of the most difficult parts of our campaign. We just spoke about the kenetic side, was a key element but only a facet and was between us and the enemy. We were comfortable with the fighting. When I say comfortable I don't mean it's easy, I just mean fighting is our profession and is our normal business and we're used to it and we're good at it. When it came to the complexity of the counter-insurgency aspect, we needed a switch in our brain which was able to flick in a fraction of a second from conventional fighting to counter-insurgency and focus on the people, from day one when we took over our area of responsibility, we focused on the population centre. I would break that down into three areas, one is the insurgent, which I've covered, the local people, and the government, but the primary focus was the local people. The only way we could build up trust was to get exposure out with the locals, working with the Afghan police and the Afghan army and this took a lot of time and a lot of risk but it was worth the risk. We went down the route of doing things like stopping at a shop and taking off our sunglasses and our helmets and we would speak to people in their own language. We learnt as much Pashtu as we could, just to break down that barrier of their perception of us as a robot with helmet, glasses and body armour. You could dehumanise us at a glance so we needed to breakdown those barriers. Our main effort was to understand the humane terrain and economic network and get in tune with everyday life.

How much of that is the intuition you have there on the ground and how much of that is training?

In the early stages of the counter-insurgency campaign in Afghanistan it was pretty, not under-developed, but we just weren't fully developed and practised in counter insurgency. We did not have intuition at the start of operations in Afghanistan, unfortunately we had forgotten a lot of our counter-insurgency mindset and skillset we had acquired from other operations such as Malaysia. It has taken almost ten years for us to build up our intuition which has now transformed us from professionals to utter professionals. In the time building and acquiring our intuition we relied heavily on our training, allowing us to survive in a hostile area until we were able to fully understand the human terrain.the right stage of the campaign, but once we had security and we were conducting the transition, we had an environment where we could speak to the people without hindrance from the enemy. There are packages that the army supply and as part of our training we do Pashtu courses, basic linguistic skills and also cultural awareness. We are very aware of Muslim societies, the Quran and we're a really multi-cultural organisation. We don't want to come across as arrogant, or indeed as the infidel that the Taliban would like to portray us as to the Afghan people.

Has your motivations for doing what you do changed at all as the conflict progressed?

I would say I have got wiser over the years and that is just an accumulation of specific knowledge in extreme circumstances. Knowledge is power so I have spent that last 12 years educating myself, and learning from experiences in deployment on operations. My fundamental motivations have not changed, I am still very much in the pursuit of being an utter professional in my field. My outlook on global terror, my outlook on things like that hasn't changed much, maybe I have a deeper understanding of the "why". The "how", is ever evolving with new technologies, social networking and as yet unknown methods. I'm now in a better position to deal with terror and I am in a better position to make decisions because of the experiences I have had in the Middle East. Global terror through my eyes is slightly different than that of a civilian, as I have witnessed terror and raw extremism in its infancy prior to its journey closer to home.

What would you say makes the perfect soldier?

For what it's worth, for me a good soldier would be someone who's clearly professionally competent in what he does, he knows the job above him and he knows the job left and right of him. They're integral to the team, but at the same time they can step up, they've got the ability to step up and they've got the mindset. I think with the soldiers we have here nowadays, there is a lot more brain power than there has been, because there has to be.

Yes your situation in Zarghun Kalay demanded that.

I would say, long gone are the days of the soldier with a rifle and "point-and-shoot", long gone are those days. Nowadays our soldiers are multi-lingual, whether that be a few sentences or a few words, their conception of counter-insurgency is second-to-none. They know that one wrong shot in a village can have devastating consequences at a strategic level in Afghanistan. But a perfect soldier? I couldn't pin it down to any single attribute.

Depends on the role to an extent.

Broadly speaking, in the Army, our greatest challenge is people. Just because of the nature of the beast, that's both subordinates and your superiors. It's a difficult one, it's one that I am still trying to get right to see what works. The greatest challenge is convincing someone that they are doing the right thing and to keep doing it every single day. Nothing's perfect, nothing is ever going to be smooth and straightforward. So the greatest challenge is doing the right thing every time.

Is there any advice you would give to someone joining the Army?

If I was to give any advice to someone joining the Army it is to have confidence in yourself, you can go through life and people can tell you what they think and most times it may be right but sometimes they are not always right and what you know is right.

Are you thinking of anything in particular?

Not anything in particular but in general, when people get set into a routine and routine becomes a habit and the habit becomes a tradition then it can be very difficult to break somebody's mindset away from that tradition in the Army. I think this new generation coming through, we are different and we are thinkers and we are good at what we do.

Tony Elliott

Founder & Chairman, Time Out Group

"People often think they can't start small, you have to be of some size. I've always advised people to aim for a niche and establish yourself in that niche and then build from there".

It is hard to believe now but finding out what was going on in the nation's capital was a difficult business in 1968. There were no dedicated listings magazines and getting to grips with the cultural scene in the city meant going through what was then called the "underground press" with such titles as *International Times, Oz* and *Gandalf's Garden*. At this time, Tony Elliott was about to go into his final year at Keele University. Seeing a gap in the market, he decided to use a £75 birthday gift from his aunt to start his own listings magazine.

Time Out would serve both the alternative environment in London as well as established culture, such as the National Theatre and the Royal Shakespeare Company. Alongside this, the publication would offer coverage and analysis of the political issues that were current in London in the 1960s and 1970s such as racial equality, police harassment and the role of the state. For the first few issues the paper ran 5000 copies and was distributed personally by Tony and his co-editor Bob Harris to retail outlets around the city.

Today the magazine not only has widespread distribution in London but it is also found in many of the world's major cities including New York, Moscow, Delhi and Hong Kong. Such is the appeal of the *Time Out* brand that the Time Out Group more often than not has overseas parties coming to them asking to operate the license for a particular region. Alongside this, a thriving web platform is becoming increasingly popular as consumers shift from print to digital.

You started *Time Out* with a £75 birthday gift from your aunt in the 1960s, could you summarise what took place between getting that £75 investment and actually printing magazines?

I think the short answer is we had credit with printers and other partners so we could run the cash-flow by not paying people to begin with, especially in the early days. I can't remember the numbers but we weren't paying for issue one until we were printing issues eight, nine and ten. Printers and staffing are the two major costs of the business and I think we stretched the tolerance of our printers at various times. So that was one point, the other thing was that, broadly speaking again, most of the initial advertisers were people who were part of the same area of interest, like record shops and record companies, cinemas and theatres. As we were new and because of the openness of the times we could go back after the first or second issue and say, "do you mind paying us, we need the money!" and most of them did give us the money and in some cases I think we started offering small discounts for early payment. We had cash-flow basically.

I guess there was a degree of sympathy from advertisers.

Not sympathy, there was mutuality of interest because the kind of people we were featuring in the magazine also turned out to be people the advertisers knew, so it was all intertwined as it is in all good media projects.

What were the major challenges facing *Time Out* as a fledgling business?

I think in our case the first major obstacle that didn't go our way was distribution. I am a veteran browser of mastheads and I remember looking at Private Eye before I started the magazine and saw it was distributed by Moore-Harness so I made a mental note to talk to them. What happened was I, and the person I was working with, Bob Harris, I think we printed 5000 copies of the first run and we just went out and we took the magazines and put them out ourselves into retail outlets. Then Moore-Harness noticed this magazine. They realised it was beginning to find a market, all be it small, so by the time that we did the third issue they took the magazine on. Our print-run then went from whatever it was we were doing, let's say 5000, and immediately went to 20,000 and we probably sold about half.

What do you think drew people to *Time Out* during its early years?

We were doing information. I always say it's an information business and it was about information from day one. I was fully connected to the way things were going at the time, a lot of the cultural changes, the new-wave, whether that was music, quite a lot of theatre was emerging, poetry, books and the only place where you could really find out about these things was what was then called the underground press. There was a newspaper called *International Times* but there was also a very good political newspaper called *Black Dwarf*, and one or two others like *Oz* and *Gandalf's Garden* and things like that. None of them were doing the information in a particularly focused or dedicated way. I was also interested in what I could do for what you might call the best of the established culture, the Royal Shakespeare Company, I think the National Theatre must have existed, there was also a lot of fringe theatre, so we had the best of the established and the best of the new. I think people took one look at the clarity of what we were doing and thought, "oh why hasn't anyone thought of doing this before?". That's what it was really. It was really plugging a need.

So it was run as a cooperative when it was first started?

No, not at all. The background to this is there was a long period from about 1972 through to 1981 where basically everybody except the very senior management were all paid the same amount of money. That started because there wasn't a lot of staff and there wasn't a lot of difference between what the so-called management were being paid and the rest of the staff. The staff then got very heavily unionised and the NUJ particularly liked using the concept of everybody getting paid the same to kind of keep everyone slightly in line. When we had the big strike in 1981 and closedown it was entirely about the principle of introducing pay-scales and the management's right to manage the company basically but it was not - I emphasise - not ever, ever, ever a cooperative.

Did commercial considerations force the magazine to drift away from what would now be considered quite a radical stance on a number of issues?

No, the magazine was always commercial, we always sought to sell as many copies as we could, we actively and aggressively went out and sold advertising. I suppose the content of the magazine has shifted over the decades because the decades have shifted frankly. If you look at the 70s, the 70s was a very political period, we had the disaster of Ted Heath and the miners' strike through to Labour government and then Thatcher coming and in the 80s it was the style decade, it was the beginning of nightclubbing etc. In the 70s you had an extremely important period of time called punk and punk people were commercial in a sense that they maximised their opportunities as was appropriate.

So the content reflected what was going on in British society?

Always, exactly, yes, there was a tension between the view of the world of some of the staff who were quite political, very political in some cases, and some others, including me. So when punk and clubbing began to emerge, some of those people didn't see that activity as being particularly something worth covering enthusiastically because they had a more censorious view of what was worth doing. That was another contributory reason as to why we had to close down and had the strike in 1981, it was that the whole rationale and direction of the way we had to do things had to change, because otherwise it would have just disappeared.

You're in the rare position of not having worked for anyone else. How important was self-employment to you and was that a major motivation for you?

I started the magazine when I was still technically at university and I was going to go away to France to study. I was aware all the time that I was working for myself and it is true that over the years I have fought very strongly to keep that independence but I think the project is more important than the idea of being self-employed because you could never have done the project without being self-employed.

How would you characterise your management style?

You'll have to ask someone else, I have no idea! I currently have a lot less to do with this than I have done, which I am very pleased about. In the period where I was much more hands-on then I could be very direct with people and be very tough and say "this is what we have to do, get on and do it". You know what has to be done and how but also I believe I have always been very open to listening to people because I didn't have much experience or knowledge to bring to the business from day one. So you solicit ideas from other people and you have to decide how much of it you are going to use.

Over the last decade or so *Time Out* has been growing extensively abroad, how have you gone about expanding *Time Out* internationally?

We've had licenses for 11 years now and it started with some people in Turkey, then people from the United Arab Emirates came to us so they did Dubai, then we had people from Israel and then from Cyprus. We organised it very quickly, having employed a consultant who knew about this area, so he went out around the world looking for other interested parties. So you reach this really virtuous point in time when you've got the critical mass where people think, "oh actually, I'm interested in doing that for my city", so they come to us.

It's really impressive that the brand has been able to maintain interest for so long and you get people coming to you from other countries.

It works very strongly because they want to do it, if you take for example Lisbon, where we have a successful licensing arrangement, the whole idea of a bunch of people from London trying to bring out a magazine in Portuguese is a non-starter.

What would be your advice to someone starting their own business?

If people have got a strong idea that is well executed, and clearly it has to be something that fulfills some kind of a need, the last thing the world needs is 150 new music magazines for example, so you've got to pick your spot, really work hard and execute it as well as possible. I think people often think they can't start small, you have to be of some size. I've always advised people to aim for a niche and establish yourself in that niche and then build from there. I think the era is over really where people have an idea that goes national and becomes enormous. It's more a question of small and good.

Tony Little

Head Master, Eton College

"Like all the powerful things in any institution, it's not what's written down, it's what's lived, it is the way people feel about a place".

Founded by Henry VI in 1440, Eton College is one of the best known schools in the UK. Successive Head Masters have fostered an ethos at the college that centres around self-reliance, achievement and a belief in being able to do great things, nurturing an impressive alumni that includes 19 Prime Ministers as well as major figures from the media, business and royalty. Tony himself is an Old Etonian, as is Sir John Gurdon, the Nobel Prize winning scientist who features later in this book.

Tony studied English Literature at Cambridge and stayed on to complete a PGCE there. He arrived at the college in 2002, having risen up through a series of headships at other schools in different parts of the country. Throughout his previous appointments, Tony developed a reputation as having a perceptive understanding of the education system as well as the strong leadership skills needed to govern a school of 1300 students.

The headship of Eton is one of the most coveted roles in education, certainly in this country, how did you get appointed to this position?

I had been a headmaster of two schools before I came to Eton so I suppose on one level I became "known on the circuit", in many more ways than one might think. I started as a headmaster at a place called Chigwell School towards the east of London, which was a very good place to start. It wasn't a particularly big school, it was in an interesting part of the world with an east-end dynamic and I was there for seven years and I then went to Oakham School in Ruckland. It was very much middle England, co-educational and predominately boarding, a very different environment of course, for six years and then I was contacted about the job.

So it's more about building up a reputation to an extent?

To an extent, I think the interesting thing is for a school like Chigwell, it is a good school, it's the sort of school that makes a good first "headship", people tend to apply out of the blue, responding to an advertisement, by the time you get to the bigger named schools, on the whole they approach you.

What did you make of the state of the British education system when you were starting out?

This was in the middle-late 1970s, it was an interesting time in a variety of ways, one of the interesting things, given what then happened, is how difficult it was for anyone to get a job. Teachers jobs were thin on the ground, wherever you looked, in the group that I was with doing the PGCE with many of them got jobs, if they got jobs, very late in the day and within ten years it was very much the other way round, schools are struggling to find people.

The PGCE course I did was, frankly, not terribly good, one of my obiding concerns in this country is the inadequacy of teacher training generally, it has become more practical over time which is a good thing but when you compare it to other national systems of education, like in Finland for example, it's a long way shy of what is needed.

Where do you feel it is failing specifically in this country?

Well I think the notion has been that you give people a shot in the arm, set them off as teachers and somehow by osmosis they work out how to do the job and there is some sense in that, if you end up in a good school in a good department, you will pick up good habits, but there hasn't been anything like the quality of training, for example, in the development of neuroscience. Very few teachers, practicing teachers I mean, are versed in the science of the brain and yet if you were to be a truly effective teacher you would understand these things. My view is that in this country you need pretty much an open house for people to experience teaching so that you can get people from different ages, different backgrounds and different professions who would consider teaching. Then after a few years if you want to continue with teaching you become a sort of chartered teacher, with a pretty stiff level of training and certification, to make it a genuine profession body. One of the problems with teaching is it calls itself a profession and it is up to point but then it isn't, it is a bit of a halfway house, by comparison, for example, with medicine or law.

There are so many different schemes now for people who want to enter teaching, how would you go about establishing yourself in the sector now?

I'll tell you I do here is I am completely relaxed with teachers coming to

Eton as to whether they have a professional qualification or not and and I am quite happy to take people who don't. I'll appoint them if they good people with good qualifications who I think will make decent school masters. Then we'll train them, we'll train them on the job and that is at least as effective as appointing someone who has a formal qualifications. That isn't a criticism of the business of being formally qualified, it is a criticism of the current situation.

So if you are not looking for qualifications, what are you looking for in a potentially respectable teacher? I know a lot of of my own teachers complained having started in teaching 20-odd years ago and it has become something it wasn't when they started out, they are being held to curriculums and the environment is becoming more clinical in their eyes.

Indeed, there is a strong truth in that. What I look for is a good academic qualification, an ability to contribute more broadly in the curriculum, or co-curriculum, which is very important in a boarding school and the other thing that is important is that whoever I am appointing actually likes young people. There is a surprising number of people in the teaching profession who really don't like kids.

Eton has been around now for 570 years, what did you want to preserve and what were you looking to change when you arrived in 2002?

The ethos of the school is pretty powerful, it wasn't exactly a broken vessel, this clearly was a successful school in all kinds of measures so in many ways it was a question of identifying what's good and making sure we stick to it rather than filling in any gapping holes. Having said that there are a number of things from which I hope we have moved on and we have touched on one of them and that is teacher training. When I arrived at Eton I came across teachers who had never had someone sit in their classrooms and watch them teach and they refused point-blank to allow people to come in, it's a culture of autonomy, and that clearly doesn't wash, and it's not good enough in my view. We now have a system of annual review, there is an appraisal, we have a system of lesson observation within departments and even across departments so you are randomly selected with someone from a completely different discipline to go and watch someone else's lesson and learn more about the art of pedagogy so that is one example. But we were in the fortunate position of having a pretty able teaching body in the first place so the trick from a leadership point-of-view, is to encourage, support and embrace the way that things have been done, but tweak and shift them gently, one hopes that when you look back over a period of time that you have come a fair way.

I'm keen to ask, because this book is primarily focused on how people have got where they are and how they achieved success in whichever area that may be, obviously Eton has got a fairly staggering track record of producing people who have gone on to do great things, what do you think it is about an education at Eton that gives someone that extra edge?

I think it's a mixture of things but perhaps I can identify four points, just to keep it succinct. First, the tradition of the place, it's largely unspoken, I am very un-keen to talk to boys about "19 Prime Ministers" and all that because it becomes self-referential and rather inward looking, so we don't need that. Nonetheless, as a teenager, you live and work in an environment where for the best part of six centuries, people have gone on to do quite extraordinary things, so it becomes part of the walk-and-weave, if you like, it becomes a level of expectation, that certain things are possible, and that's a pretty powerful environment to be in. Like all the powerful things in any institution, it's not what's written down, it's what's lived, it is the way people feel about a place.

Point two, when I talk to boys, particularly older boys who are about to leave and ask them about their views, to a surprising extent they come up with the word "excellence" and the expectation of excellence and the interesting thing is it's not so much that which is expected by teachers, it is of each other. There's a pretty strong climate within the school that they expect each other to be pretty good at whatever it is they do. It's not cool to be bad at something, whether you are writing a play, playing in a concert, whether it's your academic work, games, putting on a rock concert or running a charity function.

The third thing I would say is independence, and this is an historic thing at Eton, and something we are keen to sustain, it's this notion that you stand up for yourself and stand up for something higher than yourself and that is in a nutshell what our boys are able to do. It's structured in a way that is unusual, for example, in a boarding school of 1300 boys, each boy has his own room, there are no shared dormitories so you get an idea of being your own man in your own place. When your housemaster comes round and you're aged 13, you are talking to him man-to-man, rather than part a group of others. The tutorial arrangements we have, you are in a small group, you go to your tutor in your tutor's home. So it creates this kind of culture where people are expected to stand on their own two feet.

And the fourth element is when all these things come together, the thing that strikes me, by comparison to other schools, is you do have young men, in the main, who are the kind of people who roll up their sleeves and get things done, with an attitude of "I can do this, I can change the world", sometimes they think too much that they can change the world, but it is a good starting point. I would sum it up by saying this: enable people to have a true sense of self worth, because if you have that, then you can start being of use both to yourself and to society.

Do you have any words of wisdom for students who are deciding what to do as a career?

The kind of thing I talk to our boys about, even when they are quite young, 15 onwards, is picking up these statistics which you have now available, the figure varies but a vary significant number of them will work in jobs not yet invented and this is a huge shift, a paradigm shift in the way that schools should see what they are doing. I'm of the generation where you trained as something, like a lawyer, and there is a linear progression to 30 years later being a distinguished lawyer, or judge. For the next generation that shifted to meaning instead of having one career, you may have three or four different careers but it has shifted again and the current generation are faced with the prospect of not only having several careers but in areas that aren't even talked about yet. So you are not looking for a finite set of skills, in many ways I think the traditional liberal British education that you get at a place like Eton is even more relevant than it has been, because you are looking at those underlying qualities of character and range of skills to do with flexibility and dealing with people, the soft skills if you like, I think these are going to be even more important to the next generation than they have been for the last.

To sum it up, what I say to our boys is: the world is as it is, driven by exams, they have to get their exam certificates, nothing else matters to get into a university, that is the truth of it these days, but they also have to understand, from the moment they are at university and certainly as soon as they are in the job market all that will really matter is everything they did at school other than the stuff they did for the exam certificates and if you've got bright kids they understand that.

Yes it is about differentiating yourself to an extent.

Absolutely, as far as I am able to do so I seek to be honest with our boys, I am quite clear to them that this is the world as I see it, you can be sceptical, even cynical about exams, but they need to be able to put it in perspective.

What do you think makes a great educationist?

I think it's about passion, someone who really cares about young people, having the ability to deal with the daily and the mundane which can easily swomp you and take over the whole day while at the same time keeping your eyes on the horizon and beyond the horizon, that's the real challenge.